THE
SCIENCE
CHEF

THE SCIENCE CHEF

100
Fun Food Experiments
and Recipes for Kids

Joan D'Amico
Karen Eich Drummond, R.D.

Illustrations by Tina Cash-Walsh

JOSSEY-BASS
A Wiley Imprint
www.josseybass.com

Published by Jossey-Bass
A Wiley Imprint
989 Market Street, San Francisco, CA 94103-1741   www.josseybass.com

Published simultaneously in Canada.

Jossey-Bass books and products are available through most bookstores. To contact Jossey-Bass directly call our Customer Care Department within the U.S. at 800-956-7739, outside the U.S. at 317-572-3986, or fax 317-572-4002.

Jossey-Bass also publishes its books in a variety of electronic formats. Some content that appears in print may not be available in electronic books.

Library of Congress Cataloging-in-Publication Data

D'Amico, Joan
        The science chef: 100 fun food experiments and recipes
        for kids /
    Joan D'Amico and Karen Eich Drummond; illustrations by
    Tina Cash-Walsh
        p. cm.
        Includes index.
        ISBN 0-471-31045-X (pbk.: alk. paper)
        1. Food—Juvenile literature. 2. Cookery—Juvenile literature.
    3. Science—Experiments—Juvenile literature. [1. Food.
    2. Science—Experiments. 3. Cookery. 4. Experiments.]
    I. Drummond, Karen Eich. II. Cash-Walsh, Tina 1960– ill.
    III. Title
    TX355.D3   1995
    641.3—dc20
    94-9045

Printed in the United States of America
FIRST EDITION
PB Printing   30 29 28 27 26 25 24 23 22 21

To our children: Alexa, Caitlin, Christi, and Kyle,
and our helpers, Linda and Beth.

CONTENTS

ABOUT THIS BOOK

The Science Chef will help you learn about science in new and tasty ways. Every time you cook, you will use the science of chemistry to mix and heat ingredients to make something new, like bread from flour, yeast, and water, or popcorn from corn kernels and heat. You will learn about biology when you investigate fruits, seeds, grains, herbs, spices, and other products from nature that we eat. And you will be learning the science of nutrition when you think about how the substances in foods affect your body.

The first section, "Discovering the Kitchen," covers the basics about kitchen tools, cooking skills, and safety rules. Read it carefully before you do any of the experiments or try any of the recipes.

Part 1, "Questions, Questions, Questions," explores answers to science questions such as "Why does popcorn pop?" and "How does bread rise?"

Part 2, "No More Boxes, Cans, or Jars: Do It Yourself," invites you to make foods from scratch, instead of buying them ready-made at the store, using science to mix and change ingredients. For example, you can make your own spaghetti sauce, ice pops, and pudding mix.

Part 3, "Science in the Supermarket," looks at science in your local food store. Topics include exploring how food ripens, comparing different sweeteners, and looking at fiber in breakfast cereals.

Each chapter explores a different science topic by giving you an experiment you can do right in your kitchen, followed by easy-to-make recipes that are based on the experiment. Altogether there are over 100 experiments and recipes for you to try. Each experiment includes a purpose statement, a list of the materials you will need, the steps to follow, and an explanation of what happened and why. None of the experiments requires any previous cooking experience.

After doing the experiment, you can have some fun making one or more of the recipes. For example, learn what makes popcorn pop, then make some sensational snacks such as Trail Mix Popcorn and Rosy

Popcorn. Explore what makes toast brown, and make Old-Fashioned Cinnamon Toast or Peanut-Butter-and-Jelly French Toast Cut-Outs.

easiest

intermediate

pro

Each recipe is rated according to how much cooking experience is required. The easiest recipes, marked with one chef's hat (called a *toque*), require no previous cooking experience. Intermediate recipes, with two chef's hats, require some cooking experience. "Pro" recipes, with three chef's hats, require the most advanced cooking skills.

Always be sure you have an adult to guide you when the experiment or recipe asks you to use the oven, the stove, electrical appliances, or a sharp knife.

These recipes also:

- list the time you will need to make them, the kitchen tools you'll need, and the number of servings each recipe makes.
- use easy-to-find ingredients and standard kitchen equipment.
- are kid-tested and kid-approved.
- emphasize wholesome ingredients.

At the end of the book you'll find a glossary and sections on nutrition and food safety, including an explanation of how to read a food label and a chart listing the nutritional values of all the recipes in the book.

So get on your apron, wash your hands, roll up your sleeves, and get ready to become a science chef. We hope you have as much fun learning, cooking, and eating as we did writing this book for you!

Joan D'Amico
Wayne, New Jersey

Karen Eich Drummond
Yardley, Pennsylvania

DISCOVERING THE KITCHEN

THE SCIENCE CHEF'S TOOLS OF THE TRADE

baking pan

colander

cutting board

biscuit cutter

grater

blender

cookie sheet

electric mixer

Let's take a close look at the cooking equipment in your kitchen. These are the basic tools you'll need to do the experiments and prepare the recipes in this book. Any kitchen tools that are used in only one or two recipes are described within those recipes.

baking pan   A square or rectangular pan used for baking and cooking foods in the oven. The most common sizes are 9-inch × 13-inch and 8-inch square.

biscuit cutter   A round outline, usually made from metal, used to cut biscuits from dough.

blender   A glass or plastic cylinder with a rotating blade at the bottom. The blender has different speeds and is used for mixing, blending, grinding, and pureeing.

colander   A large perforated bowl used for rinsing food and draining pasta or other foods.

cookie sheet   A large rectangular pan with no sides or with half-inch sides, used for baking cookies and other foods.

cutting board   Made from wood or plastic, cutting boards provide a surface on which to cut foods.

electric mixer   Two beaters that rotate to mix ingredients together. Used for mashed potatoes, cake batters, and other mixing jobs.

grater   Used for shredding and grating foods such as vegetables and cheese.

knives:

- **paring knife**   A knife with a small pointed blade used for trimming and paring vegetables and fruits and other cutting jobs that don't require a larger knife. (Most recipes in this book call for a knife. You will find the paring knife works well in most situations.)

- **peeler**   A handheld tool that removes the peel from fruits and vegetables.

- **sandwich spreader**   A knife with a dull blade that is designed to spread fillings on bread.

- **table knife**   A knife used as a utensil at the table.

layer cake pans   Round metal pans used to bake layers of a cake.

loaf pan   A rectangular metal or glass pan with slanted walls. Used in both baking (for breads, for example) and cooking (for meat loaf, for example).

measuring cups   Cups with measurements (½ cup, ⅓ cup, etc.) on the sides and spouts for easy pouring.

measuring spoons   Used for measuring small amounts of foods such as spices. They come in a set of 1 tablespoon, ½ tablespoon, 1 teaspoon, ½ teaspoon, and ¼ teaspoon.

microwave dish   A dish that can safely be used in the microwave oven. The best microwave dishes say "microwave safe" on the label. Don't use metal pans, aluminum foil, plastic foam containers, brown paper bags, plastic wrap, or margarine tubs in the microwave.

mixing bowls   Round-bottomed bowls used for mixing and whipping all kinds of foods.

muffin tins   Metal or glass pans with small, round cups used for baking muffins and cupcakes.

pans:

- **frying pan** (also called a sauté pan)   Used for cooking foods, such as hamburgers or onions, in hot fat.

paring knife

sandwich spreader

layer cake pan

loaf pan

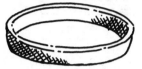

measuring cup

measuring spoons

microwave dish

muffin tin

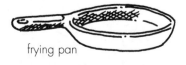

frying pan

saucepan

rolling pin

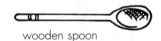

rubber spatula

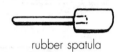

spatula

wooden spoon

steamer basket

tube pan

wire whip

- **griddle**   A flat surface without sides used for cooking pancakes, French toast, and bacon.

- **saucepan** (also called pot)   Used for general stovetop cooking, such as boiling pasta or simmering a sauce.

rolling pin   A wooden or plastic roller used to flatten items such as pie crust and biscuit dough.

rubber spatula   A flexible rubber or plastic tip on a long handle. It is used to scrape bowls, pots, and pans and for **folding** (a gentle over-and-under motion) ingredients into whipped cream or other whipped batter.

spatula   A flat metal or plastic tool used for lifting and turning meats, eggs, and other foods.

spoons:

- **teaspoon**   A spoon used for measuring. Also the name for the spoon normally used as a utensil at the table.

- **wooden spoon**   Used for mixing ingredients together and stirring.

steamer basket   A perforated metal basket used to hold vegetables or other foods so that they can be steamed in a saucepan.

tube pan   A metal cake pan with a center tube used for making angel food cakes, bundt cakes, and special breads.

wire whip   Used especially for whipping egg whites and cream.

wire rack   Used for cooling baked goods.

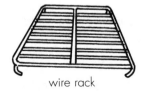

wire rack

COOKING SKILLS

Chefs need to master cutting and measuring skills and the basics of mixing and stovetop cooking. Here are the skills you will be practicing as you try the recipes in this book.

CUTTING

Foods are cut before cooking so that they will look good and cook evenly. Place the food to be cut on a cutting board and use a knife that is a comfortable size for your hand. To hold the knife, place your hand on top of the handle and fit your fingers around the handle. The grip should be secure but relaxed. In your other hand, hold the item being cut. Keep your fingertips curled under to protect them from cuts. (See the "Safety Rules" section of this chapter for more on how to cut safely.)

Here are some commonly used cutting terms you'll need to know.

chop   To cut into irregularly shaped pieces.

dice   To cut into cubes of the same size.

mince   To chop very fine.

slice   To cut into uniform slices.

Grating and shredding are also examples of cutting.

grate   To rub a food across a grater's tiny punched holes, to produce small or fine pieces of food. Hard cheeses and some vegetables are grated.

shred   To rub a food across a surface with medium to large holes or slits. Shredded foods look like strips. The cheese used for making pizza is always shredded.

chopped

diced

sliced

minced

grate

shred

Equivalents

1 tablespoon = 3 teaspoons

1 cup = 16 tablespoons

1 cup = 8 fluid ounces

1 quart = 2 pints

1 quart = 4 cups

1 quart = 32 fluid ounces

1 gallon = 4 quarts

1 stick butter or margarine
   = ½ cup = 8 tablespoons

MEASURING

Ingredients can be measured in three different ways: by counting (six apples), by measuring volume (½ cup of applesauce), or by measuring weight (a pound of apples).

To measure the volume of a liquid, always place the measuring cup on a flat surface and check that the liquid goes up to the proper line on the measuring cup while looking directly at it at eye level.

To measure the volume of a dry ingredient, such as flour, spoon it into the measuring cup and level it off with a table knife. Do not pack the cup with the dry ingredient—that is, don't press down on it to make room for more—unless the recipe says to.

MIXING

There are all kinds of mixing! Here are definitions of the most common types.

beat   To move the utensil back and forth to blend ingredients together.

cream   To mix a solid fat (usually margarine or butter) and sugar by pressing them against the bowl with the back of a spoon until they look creamy.

fold   To move the utensil with a gentle over-and-under motion.

mix   To combine ingredients so they are all evenly distributed.

whip   To beat rapidly using a circular motion, usually with a whip, to incorporate air into the mixture (such as in making whipped cream).

whisk   To beat ingredients together lightly with a wire whip until they are well blended.

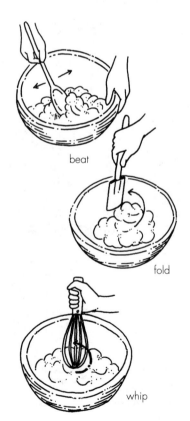

beat

fold

whip

STOVETOP COOKING

There are different ways to cook on your stove. Here are descriptions of cooking methods you will be practicing as you try the recipes in this book. Because it is easy to get burned while cooking on the stove, see the "Safety Rules" section of this chapter.

boil   To heat a liquid to its boiling point, or to cook in a boiling liquid. Water boils at 212°F (100°C). You can tell it is boiling when you see lots of large bubbles popping to the surface. When a liquid boils, it is turning into steam (the gaseous state of water). Water can't get any hotter than 212°F (100°C); it can only make steam faster. Boiling is most often used for cooking pasta.

boil

simmer

simmer   To heat a liquid to just below its boiling point, or to cook in a simmering liquid. You can tell a liquid is simmering when it has bubbles floating slowly to the surface. Most foods cooked in liquid are simmered. Always watch simmering foods closely so that they do not boil.

steam   To cook in steam. Steam has much more heat and cooks foods more quickly than boiling water does. Steaming is an excellent method for cooking most vegetables.

pan-fry   To cook in a pan over moderate heat in a small amount of fat. Hamburgers are an example of a food that can be pan-fried.

sauté   To cook quickly in a pan over medium-high heat in a small amount of fat. Vegetables, especially onions, are often sautéed in oil to bring out their flavor and brown them.

sauté

CRACKING AND SEPARATING EGGS

It is best to crack an egg into a clear glass cup (such as a measuring cup) before adding it to the other ingredients. That way if the egg smells bad or has a red spot, you can throw it out before the egg goes in with the other ingredients. An egg with a red spot is safe to eat, but is usually thrown out because of its appearance. You should also check for eggshells in the egg before adding the egg to the other ingredients.

Sometimes you will need to separate the egg yolk from the egg white for a recipe. To do this, crack the egg over an egg separator and a bowl. Make sure you get the yolk in the middle. The whites will drain out into the bowl. If you don't have an egg separator, you can separate an egg by cracking it over a bowl, keeping the yolk in one half of the shell. Carefully pass the egg yolk from one half of the shell to the other without letting it break until the whites have all fallen into the bowl.

SAFETY RULES

The kitchen can be a safe, or a very dangerous, part of your home. What's dangerous in your kitchen? Sharp knives, boiling water, and hot oil are a few things. Always check with an adult before trying any of the recipes. Talk to them about what you are allowed to do by yourself and when you need an adult's assistance. And always follow these safety guidelines.

AROUND THE STOVE AND OVEN

- Get your parent's permission before using a stove or oven.

- Don't wear long, baggy shirts or sweaters when cooking. They could catch fire.

- Never turn your back on a frying pan that contains oil.

- Never fry with oil at a high temperature.

- Don't spray a pan with vegetable oil cooking spray over the stove or near heat. Oil will burn at high temperatures, so spray the pan over the sink.

- If a fire starts in a pan on the stove, you can smother it by covering it with the pan lid or pouring baking soda on it. Never use water to put out a fire in a pan with oil—it only makes a fire worse.

- Always use pot holders or wear oven mitts when using the oven or handling something that is hot. Make sure your pot holders are not wet. Wet pot holders transmit the heat from the hot item you are holding directly to your skin.

- Don't overfill pans with boiling or simmering liquids.
- Open pan lids away from you to let steam escape safely.
- Keep pan handles turned away from the edge of the stove. They could be knocked and splatter hot food.
- Stir foods with long-handled spoons.
- Keep pets and small children away from hot stoves and ovens during cooking. (Try to keep them out of the kitchen altogether.)

USING ANY APPLIANCE

- Only use an appliance that you know exactly how to operate.
- Never operate an appliance that is near the sink or sitting in water.
- Don't use frayed electrical cords or damaged plugs and outlets. Tell an adult.

USING A MICROWAVE OVEN

- Use only microwave-safe cookware, paper towels, paper plates, or paper cups.
- Use pot holders to remove items.
- If a dish is covered, make sure there is some opening through which steam can escape during cooking.
- When taking foods out of the microwave, open the container so that steam escapes *away* from your hands and face.
- Prick foods like potatoes and hot dogs with a fork before putting them into the microwave.
- Never try to cook a whole egg in the microwave—it will burst!

USING A KNIFE

- Get your parent's permission before using any knife.
- Always pick up a knife by its handle.
- Pay attention to what you're doing!
- Cut away from the body and away from anyone near you.
- Use a sliding, back-and-forth motion when slicing foods with a knife.

- Don't leave a knife near the edge of a table. It can be easily knocked off, or a small child may touch it.
- Don't try to catch a falling knife.
- Don't use knives to cut string, or to open cans or bottles, or as a screwdriver.
- Don't put a knife into a sink full of water. Instead, put it on the drainboard, to avoid cutting yourself.

PART 1

QUESTIONS, QUESTIONS, QUESTIONS

CHAPTER 1

WHY DOES POPCORN POP?

Have you ever wondered about what would happen if you put uncooked kernels of corn from corn on the cob into the microwave? Would they pop and make great popcorn? The bad news is that they would just make a mess of your microwave. The good news is that popcorn, whose proper name is *popping corn*, is a special breed of corn that will explode to 30 to 40 times its original size when you heat it.

Only popping corn will pop. The secret to its pop is a drop of water found in each kernel. As each kernel is heated, the drop of water turns to steam (just as boiling water turns to steam). The steam is energy that breaks the hard kernel, and out pops popcorn!

Popcorn is a great snack that is easy to make, fun to eat, and low in fat (as long as you don't load it with butter). Popcorn is also a great source of fiber. Depending on how you make your popcorn and what you add to it, you can have a snack with a lot of, or just a little, fat.

Three ways to pop your popcorn are: in a hot-air popper made especially for that purpose, in hot oil using almost any type of pan, or in the microwave using specially packaged microwave popcorn.

Let's check out some fun popcorn facts! Did you know that...

- Wherever early European explorers discovered Native Americans who farmed, they found popcorn was an important food.
- Popcorn was served at the first Thanksgiving.
- Popcorn is sold in 99 percent of all movie theaters.
- The residents of the twin cities of Minneapolis and St. Paul (Minnesota) eat more popcorn per person than people do anywhere else in the United States.
- You can buy popcorn with either white or yellow kernels. White corn pops up fluffier than yellow corn, but most popcorn sold in the United States is yellow corn because it tastes better.

EXPERIMENT

HOW TO GET THE BEST POPS FROM YOUR POPCORN

Purpose

To determine whether dry or wet popcorn pops better.

Materials

1½ cups unpopped popcorn
cookie sheet
medium bowl
plastic sandwich bag
colander
frying pan, lid, and vegetable oil
    or
hot-air popcorn popper

Procedure

1. Place ½ cup popcorn on cookie sheet and leave in an oven at 200°F for 60 minutes.

2. Place ½ cup popcorn in bowl with 1 cup water for 60 minutes. After 60 minutes, drain the popcorn in a colander.

3. Leave ½ cup popcorn in a plastic bag for 60 minutes.

4. Pop each of the three batches of popcorn separately. You can use a hot-air popper or the following recipe for The Best Popcorn.

5. Which batch of popcorn made the biggest kernels of popcorn? Which batch made the smallest kernels?

6. Measure how much popcorn each batch made using a measuring cup. Which batch made the most popcorn? Which batch made the least popcorn?

What Happened?

The popcorn that was soaked in water made the biggest kernels of popped popcorn as well as the largest amount of popcorn. This is because the soaking process added water to the kernel. The more water there is, the more steam is created in cooking, making the kernels pop better. The popcorn that was dried out in the oven lost most of that drop of water that turns to steam during popping. The dried popcorn kernels made smaller kernels of popped popcorn and were more likely to be duds. Therefore they produced the smallest amount of popped popcorn. The popcorn that was left in a plastic bag made medium-sized kernels of popped popcorn and an average amount, as it was neither dried nor soaked.

•••• The Best Popcorn ••••

If you don't have a frying pan for this recipe, you can use a stockpot, a Dutch oven, or even a wok.

Ingredients

2 tablespoons vegetable oil   ½ cup unpopped popcorn kernels

Steps

1. Preheat the frying pan by placing it on the burner and setting the heat to medium for two minutes.

2. Add the oil.

3. Put one kernel into the frying pan and heat. When the kernel pops, you will know that the oil is at the right temperature.

4. Put the rest of the kernels in the pan and cover loosely with the lid.

5. During popping, shake the pan back and forth about one inch above the burner, so each kernel is heated evenly and does not burn. Continue to shake until popcorn stops popping—about 3 to 4 minutes—and remove from heat immediately.

6. Turn the burner off.

7. Slowly remove the lid so the steam escapes away from you. Let the popcorn cool for a minute, then serve in a large bowl.

Time
10 minutes

Tools
frying pan with lid

large bowl

Makes
5 2-cup servings

•••••
Don't substitute butter or margarine for the vegetable oil. Butter or margarine will burn at the temperatures used in this recipe; oil won't.
•••••

•••••
Carefully measure the popcorn. If you use too much, it will pop all over the kitchen.
•••••

•••••
Unpopped popcorn should be stored in the refrigerator to retain its moisture and give you the best "popped" results.
•••••

•••••••••••• •••• Rosy Popcorn •••• •••••••••••

Time
5 minutes to prepare
plus
1 hour to set

Tools
small microwave dish
with lid
large bowl

Makes
5 2-cup servings

•••••
Food coloring is a dye
you can eat that is
used to color foods.
•••••

This recipe is great for making a colorful and tasty gift. Just place two cups of Rosy Popcorn in a pretty disposable cup, wrap with red or clear cellophane, and tie with curling ribbon.

Ingredients

¼ cup margarine

1 teaspoon red food coloring

10 cups popped popcorn (made by popping ½ cup popcorn kernels)

Steps

1. Place margarine in the microwave dish and cover.

2. Cook the margarine on the high setting for 30 to 60 seconds until melted and bubbly.

3. Let cool for 1 minute before removing cover.

4. Add food coloring to the margarine and stir until thoroughly mixed.

5. Slowly drizzle the colored margarine over the popcorn in the bowl. Stir constantly until popcorn takes on a rosy color.

6. If wrapping up as a gift, wait one hour so it's no longer sticky.

Variation

To make popcorn with three colors, place 3⅓ cups of popcorn in each of 3 bowls. Drizzle red-colored margarine over the first bowl, green-colored margarine over the second bowl, and plain margarine over the last bowl.

Raisin Popcorn Squares

If you like raisins and soft marshmallows, try this recipe! It's a great packable snack, too.

Ingredients

½ cup margarine

1 (10½ oz.) bag mini marshmallows

¼ cup honey

10 cups popped popcorn (made by popping ½ cup popcorn kernels)

1 cup raisins

vegetable oil cooking spray

Steps

1. Preheat the frying pan by placing it on the burner and setting the heat to medium for two minutes.

2. Add the margarine.

3. Once the margarine is melted, reduce the heat to low and add the marshmallows.

4. Stir constantly until the marshmallows are melted, about 2 minutes.

5. Add the honey and stir well.

6. When the honey is all mixed in, remove the mixture from the heat and turn off the burner.

7. Let the mixture cool for 5 minutes.

8. Add the warm mixture to a large bowl filled with popped popcorn.

9. Add the raisins, stirring constantly until everything is coated.

10. Spray a cookie sheet with vegetable oil cooking spray.

11. Pour the popcorn mixture onto the sheet and press it

Time
20 minutes to prepare
plus
2 hours to set

Tools
large frying pan

large bowl

cookie sheet with 1½-inch sides

serrated knife

Makes
24 squares

• • • • •

Marshmallows are made of sugar, egg whites, and gelatin.

• • • • •

A serrated knife looks like it has teeth. The teeth prevent the food being cut from getting squashed.

down. If the mixture gets too sticky, wet your hands with cold water.

12. Allow the mixture to set in the sheet for two hours.

13. Cut with a serrated knife into squares.

Variations

Butterscotch is made by cooking margarine or butter with brown sugar.

Peanut Popcorn Squares   Use ½ cup peanut butter in place of honey in step 5. Use 1 cup peanuts in place of raisins in step 9.

Butterscotch Popcorn Squares   Use ½ cup peanut butter in place of honey in step 5. Use 1 cup peanuts and 10 ounces butterscotch morsels in place of raisins in step 9.

• • • • • • • • • • • • • • • •   Trail Mix Popcorn   • • • • • • • • • • • • •

Time
15 minutes

Tools
large bowl

plastic bags

Makes
18 1-cup servings

Sunflower seeds *are the seeds of certain varieties of the sunflower plant. Sunflowers can grow to be over 6 feet tall.*

This is a great snack to pack for bike rides, hiking, and other outdoor activities.

Ingredients

10 cups popped popcorn (made by popping ½ cup popcorn kernels)

3 cups pretzel sticks

2 cups Wheat Chex® cereal

1 cup Corn Chex® cereal

1 cup raisins

½ cup sunflower seeds

½ cup sliced almonds

Steps

1. Measure the ingredients one at a time and put them into the bowl.

2. Toss all the ingredients together. To keep Trail Mix Popcorn fresh, put it in plastic bags.

Cheddar-Cheese-and-Chive Popcorn

This recipe combines popcorn with cheddar cheese and chives for a unique flavor. Chives are an herb from the same family as onions. They have long, green leaves that look like skinny tubes and have a mild oniony flavor.

Time
15 minutes

Tools
small microwave dish with lid

large bowl

Makes
5 2-cup servings

Ingredients

¼ cup margarine

⅓ cup grated cheddar cheese

10 cups popped popcorn (made by popping ½ cup popcorn kernels)

1 bunch fresh chives
or
2 tablespoons dried chives

Steps

1. Place margarine in the microwave dish and cover with lid.

2. Cook the margarine on high for 30 to 60 seconds until the margarine is melted and bubbly.

3. Let cool for 1 minute before removing cover.

4. Add the grated cheese to the melted margarine and stir until the cheese is melted.

5. Pour the margarine-cheese mixture over the popcorn in a large bowl and toss until all the popcorn is coated.

6. If using fresh chives, wash, drain, and chop them to make ¼ cup.

7. Toss the fresh or dried chives with the popcorn mixture and serve immediately.

•••••••••••• •••• Popcorn Santa Fe •••• ••••••••••••

Time
15 minutes to prepare
plus
5 minutes to cook

Tools
frying pan

large bowl

cookie sheet
with 1½-inch sides

Makes
24 squares

This recipe is inspired by the cooking of the southwestern United States. Southwestern cooking uses some spicy seasonings such as cumin and chili powder.

Ingredients

¼ cup margarine

½ cup grated cheddar cheese

10 cups popped popcorn (made by popping ½ cup popcorn kernels)

1 teaspoon salt

½ teaspoon cumin powder

¼ teaspoon chili powder

vegetable oil cooking spray

⅔ cup grated cheddar cheese

½ cup salsa

1 bag nacho chips

• • • • •
Salsa *is a spicy sauce that is popular in Mexican cooking. It contains tomatoes, chili peppers, and other ingredients.*
• • • • •

Steps

1. Preheat the oven to 350°F.

2. Preheat the frying pan by placing on a burner and setting heat to medium for two minutes.

3. Add the margarine to the frying pan.

4. Once the margarine is melted, add the ½ cup grated cheese and stir until the cheese is melted.

5. Turn the burner off and set the frying pan on an empty burner.

6. Let the mixture cool for 5 minutes.

7. Add the margarine-cheese mixture to the popcorn in a large bowl and toss until the popcorn is coated.

8. Add the salt, cumin, and chili powder to the popcorn and toss again.

9. Spray a cookie sheet with vegetable oil cooking spray.

Spread the popcorn mixture on the cookie sheet.

10. Sprinkle the popcorn with the remaining ⅔ cup grated cheese. Spoon on salsa. The salsa will not cover all of the popcorn—just add small spoonfuls here and there.

11. Bake in the oven for 2 to 3 minutes or until the cheese has barely melted.

12. Remove the popcorn from the cookie sheet with a spatula. Serve the popcorn on top of a large platter of nacho chips with extra salsa if you like.

Holiday Popcorn Balls

Time
20 minutes to prepare
plus
1 hour to refrigerate

Tools
large frying pan

large bowl

cookie sheet with sides

plastic wrap

Makes
12 popcorn balls

•••••

Dried currants look like
small raisins and taste
sweet and tangy.
Citron is a citrus fruit
similar to lemon. Its thick
rind is candied and used
in baking.

•••••

Wrap these holiday popcorn balls with colored
cellophane, tie up with curling ribbon, and hang
as decorations or give to your friends as gifts.

Ingredients

½ cup margarine

1 (10½-oz.) bag marshmallows

¼ cup honey

10 cups popped popcorn (made by popping ½ cup popcorn kernels)

½ cup dried fruit pieces (such as chopped apples or apricots)

½ cup dried currants

½ cup shredded coconut

¼ cup chopped citron

Steps

1. Preheat the frying pan by placing it on a burner and setting the heat to medium for two minutes.
2. Add the margarine to the frying pan.
3. Once the margarine is melted, reduce the heat to low. Add the marshmallows and stir.
4. When the marshmallows are melted, add the honey and stir until melted.
5. Turn the burner off and set the frying pan on a cold burner.
6. Let the mixture cool for 5 minutes.
7. Add the melted margarine mixture to the popcorn in the large bowl and toss until the popcorn is coated.
8. Add dried fruit, currants, coconut, and citron to the popcorn mixture and mix thoroughly.
9. Moisten your hands with water. Take about ¾ cup of the popcorn mixture and pack it into a ball. Repeat until you have used up all the popcorn.
10. Place the balls on a cookie sheet. Cover them loosely with plastic wrap and refrigerate for one hour.
11. Wrap popcorn in colored cellophane and tie with decorative ribbons.

CHAPTER 2
WHY DO ONIONS MAKE YOU CRY?

Did you ever notice someone crying when he or she was chopping onions? Did you think this person was just having a bad day? Well, the truth of the matter is that onions contain oils that irritate your eyes. These oils escape into the air when the onion is cut, and your eyes start to tear to get rid of these oils.

Over the years, people have tried many tricks to keep their eyes from tearing. Unfortunately, most of these tricks don't work. Try the following experiment to see what really works.

ONION TEARS

Purpose

To find out what will prevent your eyes from tearing when you cut onions.

Materials

1 onion
knife
cutting board
matchstick
cheese
bowl of water
safety goggles or scuba mask

Procedure

1. While slicing the onion on a cutting board, try the following:

- Put a matchstick between your teeth.
- Put a piece of cheese between your teeth.
- Wear sunglasses.
- Wear safety goggles or a scuba mask.

2. Did any of these help prevent your eyes from tearing? Which one(s)?

What Happened?

The only thing that works is to shield your eyes from the obnoxious oils by wearing safety goggles or a scuba mask. That's because they keep any air (and the oils in the air) from getting to your eyes. But since the tears go away by themselves in a few minutes, most people just let them happen.

French Onion Soup

French Onion Soup is quite simple to make: just simmer onions in beef broth. A slice of toasted French bread topped with cheese usually garnishes, or decorates, this soup.

Time
25 to 30 minutes

Tools
knife

cutting board

large saucepan

Makes
4 1-cup servings

Ingredients

5 medium or 3 large yellow onions

2 tablespoons vegetable oil

2 (14½-oz.) cans beef broth

1 tablespoon Worcestershire sauce

4 ½-inch slices French bread

½ cup shredded Swiss cheese

½ cup grated Parmesan cheese

Steps

1. Remove the outer, papery skin from the onions.

2. On a cutting board, use a knife to cut the onions in half.

3. Lay each onion half flat on the cutting board and cut into ¼-inch slices.

4. Preheat the saucepan by placing on the burner and setting the heat to medium for two minutes.

5. Add the oil to the pan.

6. Add the onions and sauté about 5 minutes until golden brown and tender.

7. Add the broth and Worcestershire sauce to the pan. Simmer uncovered for 15 minutes.

8. Preheat the broiler.

9. Put the bread slices on a broiler pan.

10. Place some of both cheeses on top of each slice of bread.

11. Toast under the broiler until the cheese is lightly browned, keeping an eye constantly on the bread and cheese so it doesn't burn.

12. Ladle the soup into bowls and float one slice of bread on top of each bowl with the cheese side up.

• • • • •
For a really delicious soup, grate your own Parmesan cheese instead of using the grated cheese in the shaker.
• • • • •

CHAPTER 3

WHY DOES TOAST BROWN?

Did you ever wonder what happens in your toaster to transform ordinary white bread into brown, crispy toast? Two processes are going on in your toaster or broiler every time you turn it on. First, the heat made by the toaster dries out the water on the surface of the bread and causes it to form a dry, crispy crust. Then, the brown color of the crust develops as the sugars and starches in the bread undergo chemical changes. If you have ever heated sugar in a pan, you've seen that it turns brown when it gets hot.

Toasting means more than just toasting English muffins in your toaster. Toasting also means browning, crisping, or drying many foods by exposing them to heat. The recipes in this chapter use different pieces of equipment for toasting, including a toaster, a broiler, and a frying pan.

WHICH TOASTS FASTER?

Materials
2 slices of bread
1 tablespoon margarine
broiler pan

Procedure

1. Preheat the broiler. (Don't do this experiment in a toaster—you'll ruin the toaster!)

2. Spread the margarine on one slice of bread. Leave the other slice plain. Place both slices on a broiler pan.

3. Place the bread about 3 to 4 inches from the broiler and broil until one slice is nicely browned. Using pot holders, remove the pan from the broiler.

4. Compare the color of the two slices of bread and how much each was toasted. Which one toasted best?

What Happened?

When bread is exposed to heat, the surface dries and a crust forms. The crust browns because the protein and sugar in the bread turn darker when they are heated. If bread has margarine spread on it before toasting, the bread will be softer and not turn brown, because the fat keeps the bread from drying.

Purpose
To determine whether plain bread or bread coated with margarine toasts faster.

Nutmeg-and-Brown-Sugar Toast

Time
10 minutes

Tools
small bowl

broiler pan

sandwich spreader

Makes
2 2-slice servings

• • • • •

Always watch bread (or any other food) closely when it is under the broiler. At the broiler's high temperatures, foods can burn when you turn away even for just a minute.

• • • • •

This tastes really terrific in the morning before you go to school.

Ingredients

2 tablespoons white sugar

2 tablespoons brown sugar

¼ teaspoon ground nutmeg

4 slices whole-grain bread

4 teaspoons margarine

Steps

1. Preheat the broiler.

2. Mix together the white sugar, brown sugar, and nutmeg in a small bowl.

3. Place the bread on the broiler pan. Put the pan 6 inches from the broiler.

4. Toast until golden brown and remove pan.

5. Turn the bread over and spread 1 teaspoon of margarine on each slice.

6. Sprinkle the sugar mixture evenly over the toast.

7. Place the bread back under the broiler with the sugar mixture facing up, and remove when golden brown.

Old-Fashioned Cinnamon Toast

This is a great recipe to share with a grandparent.

Ingredients

4 tablespoons sugar

1½ teaspoons cinnamon

4 slices whole-grain bread

4 teaspoons margarine

Steps

1. Preheat the broiler.
2. Mix together the sugar and cinnamon in a small bowl.
3. Place the bread on the broiler pan. Put the pan 6 inches from the broiler.
4. Toast until golden brown and remove pan.
5. Turn the bread over and spread 1 teaspoon of margarine on each slice.
6. Sprinkle the sugar mixture evenly over the toast.
7. Place the bread back under the broiler with the sugar mixture facing up, and remove when golden brown.

Time
10 minutes

Tools
small bowl

broiler pan

sandwich spreader

Makes
4 pieces of toast

• • • • •
White bread can be substituted for whole-grain bread, but try using whole-grain bread. It provides more fiber and other nutrients than white bread and has a nice nutty flavor.
• • • • •

Peanut-Butter-and-Jelly French Toast Cut-Outs

Time
15 minutes

Tools
sandwich spreader

cookie cutters

medium bowl

frying pan

spatula

fork

Makes
4 servings

This is a tasty recipe for breakfast, lunch, or a snack.

Ingredients

4 tablespoons peanut butter

4 tablespoons jelly or jam

8 slices whole-grain bread

1 cup skim or low-fat milk

1 egg, beaten first with fork

1 teaspoon vanilla extract

2 tablespoons orange juice

½ teaspoon cinnamon

vegetable oil cooking spray

confectioners' sugar

fruit
or
pancake syrup

Steps

1. Spread peanut butter and jelly on 4 slices of bread. Lay the other 4 slices of bread on top, making 4 sandwiches.

2. Using your favorite cookie cutters, cut out shapes from your sandwiches.

3. Mix the milk, egg, vanilla extract, orange juice, and cinnamon in the bowl.

4. Spray the frying pan with vegetable oil cooking spray.

5. Put the frying pan on a burner set at medium-high and preheat for 2 minutes.

6. With a fork, dip the sandwich shapes in the egg mixture and place in the pan. When golden brown, turn the shapes over with a spatula, cooking the other side to finish.

7. Dust lightly with confectioners' sugar and serve with fruit or pancake syrup.

Variation

Cream-Cheese-and-Jelly French Toast Cut-Outs Substitute 4 ounces low-fat cream cheese (softened) for the peanut butter.

•••• Linzer Tart French Toast ••••

Linzer tarts are cookie sandwiches filled with raspberry jam. This recipe uses French toast instead of cookies. Make it on Valentine's Day and use a heart-shaped cookie cutter.

Ingredients

1½ cups skim or low-fat milk

1 egg, beaten

2 tablespoons orange juice

1 teaspoon vanilla extract

½ teaspoon cinnamon

¼ teaspoon nutmeg

¼ teaspoon ground cloves

vegetable oil cooking spray

8 slices whole-grain bread

confectioners' sugar

4 tablespoons raspberry jam

Steps

1. Mix the milk, egg, orange juice, vanilla extract, cinnamon, nutmeg, and cloves together in the bowl.

2. Spray the frying pan with vegetable oil cooking spray. Place the frying pan on a burner and preheat on medium-high for 2 minutes.

3. Dip each slice of bread into the egg mixture and place it in the pan.

4. When each slice is golden brown underneath, turn it over and cook the other side.

5. Move each slice to a cutting board with a spatula and allow to cool slightly.

6. With the cookie cutter, cut a shape in the center of each of 4 slices of bread. Dust each shape lightly with confectioners' sugar.

7. Spread the remaining 4 slices of bread with raspberry jam.

8. Assemble by placing a shaped slice on top of each slice spread with jam. Add syrup if you like.

Time
15 minutes

Tools
medium bowl

frying pan

cutting board

spatula

cookie cutter

sandwich spreader

Makes
4 servings

• • • • •

Cinnamon and nutmeg are sweet spices that are commonly used in baking. Cinnamon is actually the bark of a tropical tree, and nutmeg comes from the fruit of the nutmeg tree.

• • • • •

···Individual Fruit-and-··· Cheesecake Toast Tarts

Time
25 minutes

Tools
cutting board

knife

large bowl

wire whip
or
fork

medium bowl

handheld electric mixer

toaster

peeler

Makes
6 servings

Make this for Mom on Mother's Day
or Dad on Father's Day
for a breakfast they won't forget.

Ingredients

1 (8½-oz.) package low-fat or nonfat cream cheese

1 box (3.4 ounces) vanilla instant pudding

2 cups skim or low-fat milk

1 teaspoon vanilla extract

¼ teaspoon nutmeg

6 slices whole-grain bread

½ cup blueberries

6 large strawberries

1 kiwi

Steps

1. On a cutting board, use a knife to cut the cream cheese into small cubes. Place them in the large bowl and let stand.

2. Prepare the pudding mix by adding milk and whisking for 2 minutes in medium bowl.

3. Add vanilla extract and nutmeg to pudding.

4. Using the handheld electric mixer at medium speed, slowly add the pudding to the cream cheese until the mixture is smooth. Set aside.

5. Toast bread in a toaster until lightly browned.

6. Wash blueberries and strawberries.

7. Remove strawberry stems with a knife or strawberry huller and slice the strawberries in half on a cutting board.

8. Peel and slice the kiwi.

9. Spread the pudding mixture on the toast and top each slice with fruit.

• • • • • • • • • • • • • • **Strawberry Butter** • • • • • • • • • • • • • •

*Here's a great butter recipe
that doesn't use butter!*

Ingredients

½ cup strawberry preserves

1 cup margarine, softened

1 tablespoon confectioners' sugar

Steps

1. Beat the preserves, margarine, and sugar in the bowl with the spoon until light and fluffy.

2. Serve on toast, crackers, or biscuits.

Variations

Substitute apricot, blueberry, or raspberry preserves for strawberry preserves.

Time
10 minutes

Tools
medium bowl

wooden spoon

Makes
25 1-tablespoon servings

• • • • •
*The difference between
preserves and jelly is that
preserves are made from
whole pieces of fruit, while
jelly contains only the
juice of the fruit.*
• • • • •

Creamy Herb-and-Chive Spread

This is a tasty spread that's great on crackers for an afternoon snack.

Time
15 minutes
plus
60 minutes to warm
cream cheese

Tools
paper towels

knife

cutting board

medium bowl

wooden spoon

Makes
25 1-tablespoon servings

Ingredients

1 cup flat-leafed Italian parsley

½ cup fresh chives

1 (8½-oz.) package low-fat cream cheese

Steps

1. Wash parsley and chives and pat dry with paper towels.

2. On a cutting board, use a knife to mince parsley and chives. Set aside.

3. On a cutting board, use a knife to cut the cream cheese into small cubes. Set aside for 1 hour.

4. Put cubes into the bowl and mash them by flattening them against the sides of the bowl with the wooden spoon.

5. Add chives and parsley to the bowl. Mix it thoroughly with the cheese. Serve with crackers or spread on toast.

CHAPTER 4
WHAT'S SO SPECIAL ABOUT POTATOES?

The French call potatoes *pommes de terre,* which means *apples of the earth.* The Irish call them *praties,* and Americans sometimes call them *spuds.*

Potatoes are a much-loved food that we eat in more variations than any other vegetable. The average American eats about 55 pounds of fresh potatoes and more than 65 pounds of processed potatoes (such as frozen or fast-food French fries) each year! Potatoes are grown primarily in the middle and western states. Idaho alone produces nearly one-third of America's potatoes.

Potatoes are full of nutrients such as vitamin C and fiber and can be cooked in a zillion ways. They can be boiled in water and mashed, eaten whole, or cut up. They can be baked, steamed, roasted, or fried. They can be cooked and then used in a cold dish like potato salad.

The versatile potato also comes in many processed forms, such as frozen French fries or hash browns, canned whole potatoes, and dried flakes or granules that can be used to make mashed potatoes. The following recipes all use fresh potatoes.

EXPERIMENT ··· GROW YOUR OWN POTATO PLANT

Purpose

To learn how potato plants grow.

Materials

1 potato
medium jar with a wide opening
toothpicks

Procedure

1. Stick 4 to 6 toothpicks in a line around the middle of the potato.

2. Fill the jar with lukewarm water.

3. Position the potato in the jar resting on the toothpicks so that the bottom half of the potato rests in the water and the top half is out of the water.

4. Put the potato away from direct sunlight. In about one week, the potato will sprout leaves and roots. Now you can place your plant in a sunny location.

5. When your potato plant is between 6 and 8 inches high, you can transplant your seedling to a flowerpot.

What Happened?

Potatoes are grown not by using seeds but by planting parts of the potatoes that contain two or three eyes—the small oval-shaped depressions on the skin of the potato. From the eyes grows the handsome potato plant with its pretty white and purplish flowers.

Potatoes are actually the roots of a plant, which is why they are called a root vegetable.

•••••• •••• Basic Baked Potatoes ••••• ••••••••

Baked potatoes are one of the easiest foods to make. Just wash 'em, fork 'em, and bake 'em.

Ingredients

6 baking potatoes   seasonings

low-fat or nonfat sour cream
   or
plain yogurt

Steps

1. Preheat the oven to 400°F.

2. Scrub the potatoes with a brush under running water.

3. Prick the skins with a fork. This gives the steam that will develop inside the potato a chance to escape—otherwise, the potato might explode.

4. Place the potatoes on a rack in the middle of the oven and bake until tender, 50 to 60 minutes.

5. Using a knife on a cutting board, split each potato down the middle and top with low-fat (or nonfat) sour cream or plain yogurt mixed with your favorite seasoning, such as dried chives or dill and onion or garlic flavoring.

Variation

To microwave potatoes instead of baking them, prick them with a fork as in step 3. Arrange the potatoes on a paper towel in the microwave and allow 1 inch of space between potatoes. Avoid placing one potato in the middle surrounded by the others, because the potato in the middle will cook much more slowly. Use high power and cook 4 to 6 minutes for 1 potato, 6 to 7 minutes for 2 potatoes, and 10 to 12 minutes for 4 potatoes.

Time
10 minutes
plus
50 to 60 minutes to bake

Tools
scrub brush

fork

knife

cutting board

Makes
6 potatoes

•••••
Always pick potatoes that are firm and smooth. Avoid those that have wrinkles, dark areas, cut surfaces, sprouts, or a greenish color under the skin.

•••••
Bake potatoes directly on the oven rack for a crisp skin. Bake them in foil (or in the microwave) for a soft skin.
•••••

Broccoli-and-Cheddar Stuffed Potatoes

Time
70 minutes

Tools
scrub brush

knife

cutting board

saucepan with
steaming basket

large bowl

cookie sheet

Makes
6 stuffed potatoes

*To make stuffed potatoes, bake the potatoes
and add a filling. Then bake the potatoes
again—that's why some folks like to
call them "twice-baked."*

Ingredients

6 baking potatoes
1 bunch fresh broccoli
½ cup skim or low-fat milk
4 ounces cheddar cheese,
   shredded

⅛ teaspoon pepper
4 ounces cheddar cheese,
   shredded

• • • • •
*Broccoli **flowerets** are
the tightly packed heads
of tiny buds on top of
stalks. Both the stalks
and buds may be eaten
raw or cooked.*
• • • • •

Steps

1. Prepare the potatoes using the Basic Baked Potatoes
recipe.

2. While the potatoes are baking, wash the broccoli.

3. Using a knife on a cutting board, cut off the broccoli
flowerets.

4. Put the broccoli flowerets in a steaming basket.

5. Place the steaming basket in a saucepan with enough
water in it to just reach the bottom of the basket.

6. Put the saucepan on a burner. Set to high heat and
steam the broccoli for about 10 minutes.

7. Let the broccoli cool, then chop it into
smaller pieces using a knife on a
cutting board.

8. Using a knife, slice off the top of each
potato and scoop the pulp into a large
bowl.

9. Mash the potato pulp with a fork.

10. Add the broccoli, milk, 4 ounces of cheddar cheese, and pepper to the potato pulp. Mix.

11. Stuff the mixture back into the potatoes. Sprinkle with remaining cheddar cheese. Place the potatoes on a cookie sheet.

12. Put the cookie sheet into the oven and cook the potatoes for about 10 minutes or until the cheese is bubbly.

Variations

Mexican Chili Stuffed Potatoes   Substitute canned or homemade chili with beans for the broccoli.

Vegetable Cheese Stuffed Potatoes   Substitute 10 ounces of any frozen vegetable for the broccoli. Thaw the frozen vegetable in the refrigerator 1 day prior to making the recipe. Chop the vegetable before adding it to the potato pulp.

•••••••••••• •••• Smashed Potatoes •••• ••••••••••

Time
40 minutes

Tools
scrub brush

knife

potato peeler

cutting board

medium saucepan

colander

large bowl

potato masher
or
electric mixer

Makes
4 ½-cup servings

• • • • •
To use a potato masher,
place it over the potatoes
and push down.
Continue mashing until
the potatoes are smooth.
• • • • •

This recipe is for an old American favorite:
mashed potatoes.

Ingredients

2 medium boiling potatoes	¼ cup skim or low-fat milk
2 tablespoons margarine	dash salt

Steps

1. Scrub the potatoes with a brush under running water.

2. Remove the eyes and any decayed areas with knife.

3. Peel the potatoes.

4. Using a knife on a cutting board, cut the potatoes into quarters.

5. Put the potatoes in the saucepan and cover them with water.

6. Bring water to a boil over medium-high heat. Boil the potatoes until tender, about 20 to 30 minutes.

7. Using a colander, drain the water and put the potatoes in a large bowl.

8. Mash the potatoes with a potato masher or electric mixer.

9. Add margarine, milk, and salt to the potatoes. Use more milk for thinner smashed potatoes and less milk for thicker mashed potatoes.

•••••••••••• •••• Fabulous Baked Fries •••••••••••••

Most French fries are deep-fat fried, but this recipe gets the same crispy results by baking. This method eliminates the hazards of using hot fat and also reduces the amount of fat in the fries.

Time
25 minutes to prepare
plus
35 minutes to bake

Tools
scrub brush

knife

cutting board

large bowl

cookie sheet

spatula

paper towels

Makes
6 servings

Ingredients

4 large baking potatoes

4 tablespoons vegetable oil

¼ teaspoon garlic powder

¾ teaspoon seasoned salt

Steps

1. Preheat oven to 400°F.

2. Scrub the potatoes with a brush under running water.

3. Remove the eyes and any decayed areas with a knife.

4. Peel the potatoes if you like (but the peels taste good, too!).

5. Using a knife on a cutting board, slice the potatoes into ¼-inch slices. Then cut each slice into matchstick-sized pieces.

6. Put the potato pieces into a large bowl of water to prevent them from turning brown before the next step.

7. Once all the potatoes are cut, drain the water from the bowl, leaving the potatoes in the bowl.

8. Pour the oil over the potatoes.

9. Toss until the potatoes are well coated.

10. Place the potatoes on a cookie sheet.

11. Bake the potatoes for 15 minutes or until golden brown on one side. Turn the potatoes with a spatula and cook for another 15 minutes or until brown all over.

12. Remove the potatoes from the pan and drain on paper towels to remove any excess fat.

13. Sprinkle garlic powder and seasoned salt on fries, and toss.

Potato Skins with Cheddar and Salsa

Potato skins have become a popular appetizer. Skins are served with only a little potato pulp left in the skin.

Ingredients

4 large baking potatoes

¾ cup grated cheddar cheese

½ cup salsa

Steps

1. Preheat oven to 400°F.

2. Scrub the potatoes with a brush under running water.

3. Remove the eyes and any decayed areas with a knife.

4. Prick the potato skins with a fork.

5. Place the potatoes on a rack in the middle of the oven and bake until tender, about 50 to 60 minutes.

6. Remove potatoes from the oven. Using a knife on a cutting board, cut potatoes in half lengthwise. Let cool.

7. When cool enough to handle, scrape the white pulp of each potato half into a bowl, leave a thin layer of pulp on the skins.

8. Cut each skin into two pieces and sprinkle with cheddar cheese.

9. Top each skin with 1½ teaspoons salsa.

10. Place the skins on a cookie sheet.

11. Put the cookie sheet into the oven and cook the skins for about 12 to 15 minutes, or until the cheese is bubbly.

Time
1½ hours

Tools
scrub brush

knife

fork

cutting board

medium bowl

cookie sheet

Makes
16 skins

● ● ● ● ●
You can use the discarded pulp to make mashed potatoes by adding margarine, milk, salt, and pepper, as in the recipe for Smashed Potatoes.
● ● ● ● ●

Time
1½ hours

Tools
scrub brush

knife

fork

cutting board

large bowl

potato masher

cookie sheet

Makes
4 servings

Invite some friends for a potato supper party and see how creative they can be in making their own potato main dish.

Ingredients

4 large baking potatoes   2 to 3 tablespoons skim or low-fat milk

Steps

1. Preheat oven to 400°F.

2. Scrub the potatoes with a brush under running water.

3. Remove the eyes and any decayed areas with a knife.

4. Prick the potato skins with a fork.

5. Place the potatoes on a rack in the middle of the oven and bake until tender, about 50 to 60 minutes. Let cool enough to handle.

6. Using a knife on a cutting board, slice off the top of each potato and scoop out the pulp into a large bowl.

7. Add milk to the potatoes and mash the mixture with a hand masher. Combine fillings (see below) with the mashed potatoes to make 5 different stuffed potatoes.

8. When the potatoes are stuffed, put them on a cookie sheet and bake them in the oven for 12 to 15 minutes.

Fillings

Southwestern Potato   Cooked ground beef, diced tomato, and grated cheddar cheese. Top with seasoned bread crumbs.

Hawaiian Potato   Diced cooked ham, raisins, and grated muenster cheese. Top with a pineapple slice and a cherry.

Take-Me-Out-to-the-Ball-Game Potato   Hot dog slices, baked beans, and grated mild cheddar cheese. Top with croutons—toasted bread cubes that are usually seasoned to give them a distinctive flavor.

Popeye Potato   Cooked chicken cubes, spinach, and grated Swiss cheese. Top with bread crumbs.

Middle-Eastern Potato   Bulgur (whole-wheat grain that has been cooked, dried, and cracked into small pieces), sliced tomatoes, grated Swiss cheese, and chopped walnuts. To cook bulgur, put 1 cup in a saucepan with 2½ cups water and cook over low heat about 20 to 25 minutes.

CHAPTER 5

HOW DO SAUCES THICKEN?

Although few people bother making their own sauces, homemade sauce is worth the extra effort. A sauce is any flavorful liquid (usually thickened) that is used on foods. Most sauces are made from a liquid, a thickener, and seasonings. For example, to make cheese sauce, you might use milk, *roux* (a thickener, pronounced "roo") and grated cheese. Seasonings such as salt and pepper are also often added.

The thickener called *roux* is a mixture of flour and fat cooked together. The fat (such as margarine or butter) is melted in a frying pan, and then the flour is added and stirred until the mixture is smooth. The longer the roux is cooked, the more flavorful it will be. The roux can then be used to thicken sauces, soups, and gravies.

This chapter has two recipes for cheese sauce. The first uses a roux to make a homemade cheese sauce served over pasta.

EXPERIMENT USING ROUX TO THICKEN

Purpose

To show the difference between an ordinary liquid and a liquid thickened with a mixture of flour and fat.

Materials

2 13.5-ounce cans chicken or beef broth

2 tablespoons all-purpose flour

2 tablespoons margarine or butter

small saucepan

medium saucepan

2 wooden spoons

Procedure

1. Put a small saucepan on medium heat and empty 1 can of broth into it. Stir occasionally while doing the following steps.

2. Put a medium saucepan on low heat and melt the margarine in it.

3. Add the flour to the margarine in the medium saucepan and cook for 4 minutes. Stir frequently with wooden spoon.

4. Slowly empty the can of broth into the medium saucepan while stirring constantly. Bring the liquid to a boil over high heat, then simmer on medium heat for 10 minutes.

5. What did the broth look like in each pan at the end? Which one was thicker?

What Happened?

The broth heated with the roux was thicker than the broth heated without any flour or fat.

How does roux work? It's the flour that really does the thickening, because flour is quite starchy. Starch is a form of carbohydrate that does not dissolve in water at room temperature. However, as the water is heated, the starch granules absorb water and swell up to many times their original size. The result is a liquid that is thicker. The purpose of cooking the flour with fat is to coat the flour particles with fat and prevent them from clumping together in the liquid and making lumps.

Oodles of Noodles and Cheese

Time
35 minutes

Tools
2 large saucepans
large bowl
medium saucepan
colander
wooden spoon

Makes
8 servings

In this recipe, you make a cheese sauce from roux, milk, and cheese. The cheese sauce is served over hot pasta. Pasta is a general term for any shape of noodles, such as spaghetti or elbow macaroni. The dish can also be baked, for baked macaroni and cheese.

Ingredients

4 quarts water
1 pound elbow macaroni
4 cups skim or low-fat milk
2 cups evaporated skim milk
4 tablespoons margarine

½ cup all-purpose flour
3 cups sharp cheddar cheese, grated
1½ cups Swiss cheese, grated
3 tablespoons unflavored bread crumbs

• • • • •
For variety, substitute tricolor pasta twists for the elbow macaroni.
• • • • •

Steps

1. In a large saucepan, bring the water to a boil.

2. Add the pasta in batches, stirring after each addition.

3. Cook macaroni for about 8 minutes or until tender.

4. Place the colander in the sink and drain the macaroni. Transfer macaroni to a large bowl.

5. Add skim milk and evaporated milk to medium saucepan and place on burner. Turn to medium-high heat.

6. Bring milk just to a boil, then turn off the heat.

7. While the milk is heating, melt the margarine in a large saucepan over low heat. Cook until it's a little bubbly.

8. Add the flour to the margarine, and cook for 4 minutes over low heat, stirring frequently with a wooden spoon.

9. Slowly add the hot milk to the flour mixture, stirring constantly over low heat, until all milk has been added.

10. Add the cheeses to the saucepan and cook until the cheese melts.

11. Pour the cheese sauce over the noodles, then sprinkle with bread crumbs.

Variation

Baked Macaroni and Cheese   Follow above recipe, then bake in casserole dish in the oven for 20 to 25 minutes at 350°F until golden brown.

Simple Low-Fat Cheese Sauce

Time
20 minutes

Tools
blender

medium saucepan

Makes
4 ½-cup servings

This recipe is quick to make and great on any type of pasta.

Ingredients

1 12-oz. container low-fat cottage cheese

1 5-oz. can evaporated skim milk

½ cup shredded American or cheddar cheese

Steps

1. Combine cottage cheese and evaporated milk in a blender and process until smooth.

2. Pour the contents of blender into a medium saucepan.

3. Heat the mixture over low-medium heat, stirring constantly.

4. Add American or cheddar cheese to the hot mixture.

5. Stir until the cheese melts.

6. Pour over your favorite cooked pasta.

• • • • • •

Evaporated skim milk is made by removing about half of the water from skim milk. The milk is sterilized and sealed in cans so that it doesn't have to be refrigerated until after the can is opened.

• • • • • •

CHAPTER 6

WHY DOES A CUT APPLE TURN BROWN?

How appealing is a peeled apple that's been sitting around for a day? The answer is: Not very! Why? The peeled apple will have turned brown. When fruit is sliced, oxygen in the air reacts with chemicals in the fruit to make it turn brown. There are two ways to avoid this: the easiest is to eat the fruit right away, but you can also toss the cut-up fruit in a little bit of juice that contains vitamin C (such as orange juice).

Vitamin C prevents the fruit from turning brown, as you'll see in the following experiment.

PREVENTING BROWNED FRUIT

Purpose

To show how you can keep fruit from turning brown.

Materials

1 banana
cutting board
knife
2 small bowls
¼ cup orange juice

Procedure

1. Using a knife, slice the banana on the cutting board.
2. Place half the slices in one bowl and half in the other bowl.
3. Drizzle the orange juice over the bananas in one bowl.
4. Let the bananas stand 15 minutes.
5. Which fruit turned brown? Which didn't?

What Happened?

The fruit that turned brown was the banana without the orange juice. Vitamin C, an *antioxidant* present in orange juice, prevents the oxidation process in which oxygen in the air reacts with chemicals in the fruit to turn it brown.

• • • • • • • • • • • • • • • • • Summer Fruit Salad • • • • • • • • • • • • • • •

This recipe is called Summer Fruit Salad because some of the fruits used are available during the summer months.

Time
20 minutes

Tools
strawberry huller (optional)

knife

cutting board

large bowl

spoon
or
melon baller

Makes
6 servings

Ingredients

1 medium bunch seedless grapes

1 pint strawberries

2 bananas

½ cup orange juice

1 cantaloupe

½ cup coconut, shredded

Steps

1. Wash and dry the grapes and strawberries.

2. Remove the stems from strawberries with a knife or strawberry huller.

3. Using a knife on a cutting board, cut the strawberries into bite-sized pieces, and slice the bananas.

4. Place the strawberries and bananas in the large bowl with the orange juice. Toss the fruit with the orange juice to coat all the fruit.

5. Using a knife on a cutting board, cut the cantaloupe in half and remove the seeds.

6. Using a spoon or a melon baller (a tool that looks like a tiny ice-cream scoop), scoop out melon balls and place them in the bowl with the other fruit.

7. Sprinkle the coconut over the fruit.

• • • • •
One medium coconut makes 3 cups of shredded coconut.
• • • • •

•••••••••• •••• Winter Fruit Salad •••• ••••••••••

Time
20 minutes

Tools
knife

cutting board

large bowl

Makes
6 servings

This recipe uses fruits that are usually available in the winter months.

Ingredients

1 small bunch seedless grapes	1 banana
1 apple	1 tangerine
1 pear	1 cup mini marshmallows
¼ cup orange juice	⅓ cup walnuts, chopped

Steps

1. Wash and dry the grapes, apple, and pear.

2. Using a knife on a cutting board, slice the grapes in half.

3. Cut the apple and the pear into bite-sized pieces.

4. Place the fruit in a large bowl and add the orange juice. Toss the fruit with the orange juice to coat all the fruit.

5. Peel and slice the banana and place it in the bowl of fruit. Toss to coat.

6. Remove the peel of the tangerine and separate it into sections by hand. Place the tangerine sections in the bowl of fruit.

7. Sprinkle the mini marshmallows and chopped walnuts over the fruit.

···· Refrigerator Fruit Salad ····

To make this fruit salad, open the refrigerator and grab all the fruit you can get your hands on! Then check the kitchen counter to see if there is any more fruit lurking there.

Time
20 minutes

Tools
cutting board

knife

large bowl

Ingredients

an assortment of any kind of fruit, such as apples, bananas, oranges, pears, peaches, plums, berries, or melons

¼ cup orange juice

honey

mini marshmallows

shredded coconut

Steps

1. Wash the fruit.

2. Using a knife on a cutting board, chop the fruit into bite-sized pieces.

3. Put the fruit in a bowl and toss with a small amount of orange juice.

4. Top with as much honey, mini marshmallows, and coconut as you like.

•••••••••••••••• •••• **Fruit Kabobs** ••••••••••••••

Time
20 minutes

Tools
strawberry huller (optional)

knife

cutting board

small bowl

10 kabob sticks (they look like long toothpicks)

Makes
10 kabobs

This recipe is not only fun to make but fun to eat.

Ingredients

20 strawberries

20 grapes

2 apples

¼ cup orange juice

20 pineapple chunks
(if canned, drain well first)

10 marshmallows

Steps

1. Wash and dry the strawberries, grapes, and apples.

2. Remove the stems of the strawberries with a knife or strawberry huller.

3. Using a knife on a cutting board, cut 20 bite-sized apple chunks.

4. Coat the apple chunks with orange juice in small bowl. Drain.

5. To make kabobs, pierce each fruit with the pointed end of the kabob and slide it up. You can put the fruit on in any order, but here is our favorite:

1. grape

2. apple

3. strawberry

4. pineapple

5. marshmallow

6. repeat #1–4

CHAPTER 7

HOW DOES BREAD RISE?

Yeast breads are one of the world's favorite foods. Breads go with virtually any meal. They're also very simple, using just a few ingredients; mainly flour, water, sugar, and yeast. **Yeast** is a fungus that makes bread dough rise (expand). It feeds on the sugar, then gives out carbon dioxide gas. The gas gets trapped in the dough and makes it rise. When the dough is cooked, the trapped gas leaves the little holes you see in bread that give it its nice soft texture.

This chapter includes some recipes for bread dough, but first you need to know some basic rules about growing yeast, and about proofing yeast and kneading, punching, and shaping dough.

PROOFING THE YEAST

The first step in using yeast is **proofing,** which means dissolving the yeast in warm liquid, usually water. You have to take care not to kill the yeast by using water that is too hot. Yeast grows best in liquid that is between 100°F and 110°F. If the water is too cold, it will take longer for the yeast to grow, and the bread will not rise as much. If you do not have a thermometer to check the exact temperature, put some water on your wrist and make sure it feels warm, not hot.

MIXING THE DOUGH

After you've started the yeast growing in warm water, put together your ingredients and stir them into a ball of dough. The dough should be a little sticky, but not so sticky that you can't get it off your fingers. When a dough is too sticky, you need to add a little more flour.

KNEADING THE DOUGH

Once the dough is just right, place it on a lightly floured board or table for kneading. **Kneading** is the process of working dough into a smooth mass by pressing and folding. This develops the **gluten** (an elastic substance in flour that gives bread its sturdy structure) and mixes the ingredients. Kneading is important for the bread to have the right texture.

To knead, follow these steps:

1. Place the ball of dough in front of you and bring the top half of the dough over towards you.

2. Turn the dough a quarter turn, and repeat the process.

3. Continue turning the dough a quarter turn and repeating the kneading process until the dough is very soft. If the dough feels sticky, add a sprinkling of flour.

LETTING THE DOUGH RISE

After the dough is kneaded, place it in a lightly greased bowl, cover the bowl with a clean, damp towel, and put the bowl in a warm, draft-free area. Let the dough rest and rise until double in size. During rising the yeast eats the sugars and makes the carbon dioxide gas.

PUNCHING THE DOUGH

When the dough has risen (usually it takes about 1 to 1½ hours for bread), test it by inserting your fingers in the dough to the first knuckle in several places. If the finger marks close very slowly, the dough is ready to be punched—which does not mean that you hit the dough with your fist! To punch the dough, pull it up on all sides, fold over the center, and press down. Punching keeps the dough at an even temperature, expels the gas, further develops the gluten, and brings fresh oxygen to the yeast cells so they make more gas.

SHAPING THE DOUGH

Once the dough is punched, divide it (if necessary), shape into desired shapes (rolls, loaves), and place onto nonstick or lightly oiled sheet pans or other baking dishes. Let the dough rise again, until double in bulk. A fully risen loaf of dough when touched gently will slowly fill out the dents made by the fingers.

After the second rising, place directly into a preheated oven and bake until the bread is browned and sounds hollow when tapped.

To save time, you can buy frozen bread dough (usually in one-pound loaves) at the supermarket that is ready to rise and be baked. Some people also have bread machines that do all the work for you. But it's much more fun to do it by hand!

GROWING YEAST

Purpose

To compare the growth of yeast in hot, warm, and cold water.

Materials

3 packages active dry yeast

3 teaspoons sugar

3 small bowls

Procedure

1. Place the contents of 1 package of active dry yeast and 1 teaspoon of sugar in each bowl.

2. Add 1 cup of very hot water to the first bowl, 1 cup of warm water to the second bowl, and 1 cup of ice-cold water to the third bowl.

3. Look to see if the yeast are producing bubbles of carbon dioxide gas in any of the bowls.

What Happened?

Yeast will be killed by very hot water, so you are unlikely to see bubbles being produced in the bowl with hot water. You probably won't see any bubbles in the bowl with cold water, because yeast grows best in warm water (about 100°F to 110°F).

White Bread

Try this recipe on a rainy day when you will be at home most of the day.

Time
4½ hours

Tools
thermometer
large bowl
large spoon
kitchen towel
medium bowl
2 loaf pans

Makes
2 loaves (24 slices each)

Ingredients

2 cups warm water
1 package active dry yeast
1 tablespoon sugar
1 tablespoon salt
5½ to 6 cups all-purpose flour
vegetable oil

Steps

1. Put the water in a large bowl. Using a thermometer, make sure the water temperature is between 100°F and 110°F so you don't kill (or chill) the yeast.

2. Add the yeast to the water and stir. Let sit for 5 minutes.

3. Add the sugar and salt to the water and stir well.

4. Add the flour to the bowl in small amounts and stir well after each addition. Add just enough flour so the dough is not sticking in clumps to your hands or the bowl.

5. Knead the dough on a lightly floured surface for 4 minutes. Knead by pressing the dough out, then folding it in half. Give the dough a quarter turn after each fold and start again.

6. Form the dough into a ball and place it in a medium bowl that you have lightly coated with vegetable oil. Turn the dough over in the bowl so the dough has a thin layer of oil on it.

7. Cover the bowl with a damp towel and put the bowl in a warm place for 1 to 2 hours for the dough to rise.

8. When you can poke your finger in the dough without it springing back, it is time to punch the dough. To punch the dough, pull it up on all sides, fold it over the center,

*****
Active dry yeast *is dried granules of yeast that become active when put into water. It comes in small sealed packets.*
*****

and press down. Knead out all the bubbles for
1 minute.

9. Cut the dough in half. Shape it into two loaves by
rolling and patting each piece of dough to fit the
loaf pan.

10. Place the dough in loaf pans and cover with damp
towel. Let rise until double in size, about 1 hour.

11. Bake for about 30 to 40 minutes at 350°F until the
bread is browned and sounds hollow when tapped.

Basic Pizza Dough

Pizza dough is made like bread dough but doesn't have to rise, so it is ready to use in just 25 minutes.

Ingredients

1 cup warm water

1 package active dry yeast

1 teaspoon sugar

1 teaspoon salt

2 tablespoons oil

2 to 3 cups all-purpose or whole-wheat flour

Steps

1. Using a thermometer, make sure the water temperature is between 100°F and 110°F so you don't kill (or chill) the yeast.

2. Add the yeast to the water and stir.

3. Add the sugar, salt, and oil to the water and stir well.

4. Add the flour to the bowl in small amounts and stir well after each addition. Add just enough flour so the dough is not sticking in clumps to your hands or the bowl.

5. Using your hands, knead dough for 2 to 3 minutes on a lightly floured surface.

6. Let the dough rest 5 to 10 minutes before using.

Time
25 minutes

Tools
thermometer

large bowl

large spoon

Makes
1 ball of pizza dough
(enough for
1 12-inch pizza
or
8 slices)

Possibilities Pizza

Time
35 to 45 minutes

Tools
cutting board

knife

frying pan

wooden spoon

12-inch pizza pan

Makes
8 slices

• • • • •
*Sautéeing the vegetables
helps develop their
flavor and color.*
• • • • •

*Use Basic Pizza Dough to make your
own signature pizza.*

Ingredients

1 cup sliced vegetables such as mushrooms, green peppers, onions, or broccoli

1 tablespoon vegetable oil

1 recipe Basic Pizza Dough

1 jar (15½-oz.) pizza sauce

6 oz. shredded part-skim mozzarella cheese

¼ cup sliced olives (optional)

Steps

1. Preheat oven to 425°F.

2. Wash the vegetables and, using a knife, slice them on a cutting board.

3. Preheat a frying pan by placing it on a burner and setting heat to medium for two minutes.

4. Add the oil.

5. Add the vegetables and sauté for 3 minutes.

6. Press the dough evenly onto the pizza pan. (Or you can use a 13-by-9-inch baking pan to make a deep-dish pizza.)

7. Spread pizza sauce, then vegetables, then shredded cheese, and olives (if desired) on the dough.

8. Bake the pizza at 425°F for 20 to 25 minutes until the crust is lightly browned and the cheese is bubbly.

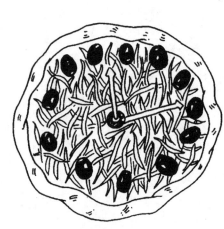

·····Stromboli Pizzoli·····

Stromboli has the same ingredients as pizza, only it is rolled up.

Time
10 minutes to prepare
plus
35 to 40 minutes to bake

Tools
cookie sheet

Makes
8 slices

Ingredients

1 recipe Basic Pizza Dough
1 tablespoon olive oil
¼ cup pizza sauce
4 oz. mozzarella cheese, grated

4 oz. pepperoni slices
vegetable oil cooking spray
2 teaspoons olive oil

Steps

1. Preheat oven to 375°F.

2. On a floured surface, pat the pizza dough into a rectangle measuring about 11 × 14 inches.

3. Brush the dough lightly with the tablespoon of olive oil.

4. Spread the sauce on the dough, leaving a ¼-inch border all around.

5. Sprinkle on the cheese.

6. Lay the pepperoni slices on the cheese.

7. Roll up the dough lengthwise like a jelly roll, and close the ends tightly.

8. Spray a cookie sheet with cooking spray.

9. Place the stromboli on the sheet.

10. Cut 3 slits in the top of the stromboli for steam to escape.

11. Brush lightly with the 2 teaspoons of olive oil.

12. Bake stromboli at 375°F for 35 to 40 minutes or until golden brown.

13. Remove from oven. Allow to cool 5 minutes, then cut into 8 slices and serve.

• • • • • • • • • • Monkey Bread • • • • • • • • • • •

Time
25 minutes to prepare,
30 minutes to rise,
and
60 minutes to bake

Tools
10-inch tube cake pan

small bowl

kitchen towel

Makes
15 servings

• • • • •
*A tube pan is a special
metal cake pan with a
center tube used for
making angel food cakes,
bundt cakes, and
special breads.*
• • • • •

*Monkey Bread is fun to make and
is pulled apart to be eaten.*

Ingredients

1 tablespoon shortening
1 cup light brown sugar
¾ cup white sugar
1 teaspoon cinnamon
flour for dusting

3 loaves frozen bread dough
   (allow to thaw and rise
   according to instructions on
   package)
      or
1½ recipe White Bread dough
¾ cup margarine, melted

Steps

1. Grease a 10-inch tube cake pan with shortening.

2. Pack the light brown sugar into a measuring cup. Combine the brown sugar, white sugar, and cinnamon in a small bowl. Mix well.

3. With flour-dusted hands, tear off 1½-inch pieces of dough. Roll each piece into a ball.

4. Dip each dough ball into the margarine, then roll in the cinnamon-sugar mixture until completely coated.

5. Place each ball in the tube pan.

6. Continue to coat the balls and place in the pan about ½ inch apart, building up layers until the dough is used or the pan is about three-quarters full.

7. Cover the pan with a clean, damp kitchen towel and let stand in a warm place until the dough rises to the top of the pan, about 30 minutes.

8. Preheat the oven to 350°F.

9. Put the pan in the oven and bake for 60 minutes, covering loosely with foil if the top begins to get too brown.

10. Remove the bread from the oven and let cool for 5 to 10 minutes.

11. Turn the bread pan upside down, holding one hand under the bread. Let the bread slip out of the pan.

12. Serve the bread warm. To eat, pull the loaf apart.

CHAPTER 8
WHAT IS BAKING POWDER?

Take a teaspoon of baking powder and add it to a cup of warm water. What happens? The baking powder makes the water bubble. Baking powder contains baking soda (a base) and an acid. *Acids* and *bases* are chemical compounds with a sour taste that react together. In the presence of heat or moisture, the baking soda reacts with the acid to produce carbon dioxide bubbles (the same as those you see in soft drinks and carbonated water). In baked goods, the bubbles swell the food being baked, resulting in, for example, cupcakes that rise.

Baking powder is used in most baking recipes that don't rely on yeast (see Chapter 7). Yeast is a live organism that is commonly used in making bread. It also produces carbon dioxide bubbles. Baking powder is used to make most cakes, cookies, biscuits, and quick breads.

Quick breads are just what the name implies—breads made quickly! This category includes muffins, pancakes, waffles, loaf breads such as banana bread, and biscuits. While white bread and whole-wheat bread require yeast to make them rise (which takes a lot of time), quick breads generally use baking powder, which causes them to rise rapidly in the oven.

Making muffins is easy. Just pay attention to these baking tips.

- Don't overbeat muffin batter or the muffins will have tunnels inside them.

- Once the batter is ready, put it into pans and bake right away. Baking powder starts its activity as soon as the batter is made, so it's important to get the muffins into the oven as soon as possible.

- Fill the muffin tins evenly and put a little water in any empty cups.
- Bake in the top third of the oven so the bottoms do not burn and the muffins cook evenly.
- Bake until golden brown and a wooden toothpick inserted into the center comes out clean. Overbaked muffins are dry.
- Let muffins cool for 5 minutes before you remove them from the pan. Always use a pot holder when you do this: simply turn the pan upside-down over a cooling rack.

BUBBLY BUBBLES

EXPERIMENT

Materials

1 teaspoon double-acting baking powder

1-quart glass measuring cup

Purpose

To show how double-acting baking powder works.

Procedure

1. Put ½ cup warm water in 1-quart measuring cup. Add the baking powder to the cup. What happens when you mix the baking powder and warm water?

2. Next, put the measuring cup into a microwave oven and microwave on high for 60 seconds. Using a pot holder, remove the cup from the microwave oven. What is happening now?

What Happened?

In this experiment, you saw that baking powder makes carbon dioxide bubbles when mixed with water and keeps making bubbles when heated. This is why the baking powder you use is called double-acting. It works when you mix your recipe and again when you cook it.

Baking Powder Biscuits

Time
35 minutes

Tools
medium bowl

2 table knives

2-inch round biscuit cutter
or
juice glass

cookie sheet

Makes
12 biscuits

• • • • •

Knead for only about 30 seconds. The dough should be soft and a little stretchy, but not sticky. Overkneading toughens the biscuits, so don't overdo it.

• • • • •

Serve these biscuits warm with honey, apple butter, or jam.

Ingredients

2 cups all-purpose flour

1 tablespoon baking powder

½ teaspoon baking soda

¼ teaspoon salt

¼ cup margarine, chilled

¾ cup low-fat buttermilk

Steps

1. Preheat oven to 400°F.

2. Combine the flour, baking powder, baking soda, and salt in a medium bowl.

3. Put the margarine in the bowl. Holding a table knife in each hand, draw the knives across each other to cut through the margarine and dry ingredients. Keep cutting until the flour and fat mixture is in pieces about the shape of peas.

4. Stir in the buttermilk just until the dry ingredients are moistened.

5. Knead the dough on a lightly floured surface 5 times. Knead by pressing it out, then folding it in half. Give the dough a quarter turn after each fold and start again.

6. Pat the dough out to a ½-inch thickness. Cut biscuits out with a 2-inch round cutter (or use a juice glass).

7. Place biscuits 1 inch apart on an ungreased cookie sheet. Bake 10 to 12 minutes at 400°F or until golden brown.

8. Remove from oven and let cool for a few minutes before serving.

•••• Blueberry Bear ••••
Pancakes

Nutritious and delicious, these pancakes will satisfy a breakfast or lunchtime appetite.

Ingredients

1½ cups all-purpose flour

½ teaspoon salt

3 tablespoons sugar

1¾ teaspoons baking powder

2 eggs

3 tablespoons margarine

1¾ cups buttermilk

¾ cup fresh blueberries, washed and patted dry

vegetable oil

Steps

1. Mix the flour, salt, sugar, and baking powder in a medium bowl.

2. Crack the eggs into a small bowl and beat lightly with a fork.

3. Place the margarine in a microwave dish, cover, and cook on high for 30 to 60 seconds until melted and bubbly. Let cool for 1 minute before removing cover.

4. Add eggs, margarine, and buttermilk to the flour mixture. Stir just until blended.

5. Add blueberries by folding (over-and-under motion) them gently into the batter.

6. Brush a griddle or frying pan with oil.

7. Place the griddle or frying pan on a burner and heat on medium.

8. Pour enough batter into the griddle or frying pan to make one 3-inch pancake. Then pour two smaller pancakes attached to the upper edge of the first pancake so that they look like ears. Cook until bubbles appear and the pancake is golden underneath.

9. Carefully turn the bear cake with a spatula. Cook the other side until golden brown, about 1 minute.

10. Serve with syrup or jelly.

Time
20 minutes

Tools
medium bowl

small bowl

fork

small microwave dish with lid

griddle or frying pan

spatula

Makes
15 pancakes

• • • • •

*Overmixing pancake batter produces tough pancakes. Stir just until the dry ingredients seem mixed in with the wet ingredients. The batter should still be a little lumpy, **not** perfectly smooth.*

• • • • •

Basic Muffins

Time
15 minutes to prepare
plus
20 to 25 minutes to bake

Tools
muffin pan

large bowl

medium bowl

wooden spoon

large spoon

rubber spatula

Makes
12 muffins

Try this recipe as is, or be adventurous and try one of the variations.

Ingredients

1 tablespoon shortening

2 cups all-purpose flour

¼ cup sugar

1 tablespoon baking powder

¼ teaspoon salt

1 egg

1 cup skim or low-fat milk

¼ cup vegetable oil

Steps

1. Preheat oven to 400°F.

2. Grease bottoms and sides of muffin cups with shortening or use a nonstick muffin pan.

3. Mix the flour, sugar, baking powder, and salt in a large bowl.

4. Mix the egg, milk, and vegetable oil in a medium bowl.

5. Add milk mixture all at once to the large bowl with the flour mixture.

6. Combine ingredients with wooden spoon just until all dry ingredients are moistened.

7. Using a large spoon, fill each muffin cup two-thirds full with batter.

8. Bake for 20 to 25 minutes at 400°F or until golden brown.

9. Remove from oven and place on wire rack. Let cool for 5 minutes.

10. Loosen muffins with rubber spatula and remove from pan.

Variations

Apple-Cinnamon Muffins   Add 1 teaspoon cinnamon and 1 cup chopped apple in step 2.

Chocolate Chip Muffins   Add ⅔ cup miniature chocolate chips in step 2.

Banana Muffins   Add 1 cup mashed banana in step 4.

Blueberry Muffins   Add 1 cup washed and dried blueberries in step 4.

Oatmeal-Raisin Muffins   Replace 1 cup of flour in step 2 with 1 cup oatmeal, and add ½ cup raisins in step 4.

Peanut-Butter-and-Jelly Muffins   Spoon half the batter among 12 muffin cups. Place about 1 teaspoon peanut butter and ½ teaspoon jelly in each muffin cup. Cover each cup with remaining batter.

Whole-Wheat Muffins   Replace 1 cup of all-purpose flour with ¾ cup whole-wheat flour in step 2.

CHAPTER 9
WHAT HAPPENS WHEN YOU BEAT EGG WHITES?

It can be amazing to see how liquidy egg whites can become light and fluffy and expand to many times their original size. When you beat egg whites (cooks like to call this whipping rather than beating) with a mixer or a wire whip, you are actually beating air into them. The egg whites stretch but hold together, trapping the air inside them. The normally compact proteins found in egg whites unfold when whipped. This also makes egg whites look fluffy.

Beaten egg whites are used to give lightness and rising power to some cakes, pancakes, waffles, and souffles (a light, fluffy baked egg dish).

Some rules to follow whenever beating egg whites:

1. When separating the egg white from the yolk, be sure the yolk does not get in the whites. Yolks contain fat, and fat keeps egg whites from being well whipped.

2. Make sure the equipment you use to whip egg whites (such as the bowl and mixer) is perfectly clean. A glass or metal mixing bowl is better than plastic because fat sometimes gets trapped in scratches on the sides of plastic bowls.

3. Egg whites whip better at room temperature. Remove eggs from the refrigerator about 1 hour before whipping.

4. Add a small amount of cream of tartar or lemon juice to egg whites to increase their volume when beaten.

5. Do not overbeat egg whites. For most recipes you should stop when the whites just hold a peak when you lift the beater up. If you overbeat egg whites, they go from being moist to being dry.

BIGGER-AND-BETTER WHIPPED EGG WHITES

Materials

3 eggs at room temperature

3 eggs at refrigerator temperature

egg separator

electric mixer

2 mixing bowls

Purpose

To determine which whips faster: chilled egg whites or egg whites at room temperature.

Procedure

1. Using an egg separator, separate the 3 room-temperature eggs. Beat using an electric mixer until stiff peaks form.

2. Repeat step 1 using the chilled eggs.

3. Which set of egg whites whipped bigger and better?

What Happened?

The egg whites that are chilled whip up to about the same volume as, or a little less than, the room temperature egg whites, but egg whites that are at room temperature can be beaten more quickly than those that are chilled.

Meringue Shells

Time
20 minutes to prepare
plus 1 hour to bake

Tools
cookie sheet

medium bowl

hand-held
or
electric mixer

spoon

cookie sheet

Makes
12 4-inch shells

• • • • •
Cream of tartar *is a
white, powdery acid found
in grape juice after
fermentation. It is beaten
into egg whites because it
makes the egg whites
firmer and sturdier.*
• • • • •

*Meringue is a mixture of egg whites and sugar
that is baked. Meringue is a popular topping
on pies, particularly lemon meringue pies.*

Ingredients

vegetable oil cooking spray

3 eggs

1 teaspoon cream of tartar

⅔ cup sugar

½ teaspoon vanilla extract

Steps

1. Preheat oven to 275°F.

2. Lightly spray a cookie sheet with vegetable oil cooking spray.

3. Crack eggs and, using an egg separator, separate whites from yolks. Place egg whites in a medium bowl.

4. Sprinkle the cream of tartar over the egg whites.

5. Beat using a hand-held or electric mixer until foamy.

6. Add sugar slowly and beat until stiff, glossy peaks appear and the sugar is completely dissolved.

7. Add the vanilla extract and beat 1 minute more.

8. Shape egg whites into twelve 4-inch diameter balls on the cookie sheet.

9. Form the balls into shells by making a depression in the middle of each ball with the back of a spoon.

10. Bake for 1 hour at 275°F or until dry and a light, creamy color.

11. Let cool 10 minutes, then remove carefully from pan.

12. Once cooled, fill with fresh fruit, canned fruit, ice milk, sherbet, or flavored ice.

Angel Food Cake

Angel food cake is a moist, airy cake with a sweet, delicate flavor. The stiffly beaten egg whites allow the cake to rise without baking powder. It contains no fat.

Ingredients

12 eggs
1 cup cake flour
¾ cup confectioners' sugar
1 teaspoon cream of tartar
½ teaspoon salt

¾ cup confectioners' sugar
1 teaspoon vanilla extract
½ teaspoon almond extract
1 teaspoon lemon juice

Steps

1. Remove eggs from refrigerator 30 minutes before starting this recipe.

2. Preheat the oven to 325°F.

3. Stir the flour and ¾ cup sugar together in small bowl.

4. Crack eggs and, using an egg separator, separate whites from yolks. Place egg whites in a large, clean bowl.

5. Sprinkle the cream of tartar and salt over the egg whites.

6. Beat using a hand-held or electric mixer until stiff peaks form. The egg whites should be shiny and moist.

7. Sprinkle some of the confectioners' sugar over the whites and gently fold in (over-and-under motion) with a rubber spatula. Repeat until all the sugar is mixed in.

8. Sprinkle the flour-sugar mixture on the egg whites and gently fold in. Repeat until all the flour and sugar is mixed in.

Time
30 minutes to prepare,
1 hour to bake

Tools
small bowl

egg separator

large bowl

hand-held
or
electric mixer

rubber spatula

10-inch tube pan

oven mitts
or
pot holders

metal spatula

12-ounce glass
soft-drink bottle

Makes
1 cake, 12 servings

• • • • •
Cake flour looks and feels softer than all-purpose flour. Cake flour contains less protein than all-purpose flour, so cakes are more tender.
• • • • •

9. Fold in the vanilla and almond extracts and the lemon juice.

10. Gently fill an ungreased 10-inch tube pan with the batter.

11. Bake for one hour at 325°F. Test by pressing lightly in the center. The cake should spring back if it is done. If not, test at 5-minute intervals.

12. With oven mitts or pot holders, remove the cake from the oven and turn the pan over onto the neck of a glass (not plastic) bottle. Let the cake cool for 1½ hours.

13. When completely cooled, remove the cake from the pan by loosening the sides with a metal spatula.

Fluffy Omelet

To make a fluffy omelet, first whip the egg whites—that will make the omelet lighter.

Ingredients

2 eggs

1 tablespoon skim or low-fat milk

vegetable oil cooking spray

Steps

1. Remove eggs from refrigerator 30 minutes before starting this recipe.

2. Crack eggs and, using an egg separator, separate whites from yolks. Put whites in a medium bowl and yolks in a small bowl.

3. Beat egg whites until stiff peaks form. The egg whites should be shiny and moist.

4. Beat yolks with a fork and add milk.

5. Gently fold egg whites into yolk mixture using a rubber spatula.

6. Spray a small frying pan.

7. Heat the frying pan over low heat.

8. Pour the eggs into the frying pan. Cook until the eggs are no longer liquid, then fold in half and cook for 2 minutes longer. Remove from the pan with the spatula.

Time
20 to 25 minutes

Tools
egg separator

medium bowl

small bowl

hand-held
or
electric mixer

fork

rubber spatula

frying pan

Makes
1 omelet

Variation

You can fill an omelet with almost anything you like. Just add the ingredient(s) before you fold the omelet in half. Here are some suggested fillings: grated cheese, chopped green peppers, diced onions, sliced mushrooms, and chopped ham or turkey.

PART 2

O MORE BOXES, CANS, OR JARS: DO IT YOURSELF!

CHAPTER 10

MAKE-YOUR-OWN SALAD DRESSINGS

Salad dressings are liquids used to flavor and moisten salads. Many salad dressings are made of a vegetable oil and vinegar and herbs and spices. Vegetable oils commonly used in salad dressings include olive oil, soybean oil, and corn oil. Vinegar and lemon juice are acidic and sour tasting. They make the salad dressing tangy.

Oil and vinegar (or lemon juice) are substances that will not mix by themselves. When you shake them together, however, they will form a *suspension,* which means that the oil will separate into small drops that will stay evenly mixed through the dressing for a short time. This is why everyone shakes salad dressing bottles before using them. When you put the salad dressing bottle down and let it sit, the oil droplets once again cling together and separate from the vinegar.

Other salad dressings use mayonnaise instead of oil and vinegar (such as Russian and Thousand-Island dressings). Mayonnaise-based dressings are thicker and creamier than those using oil and vinegar. Mayonnaise is made from egg yolks, vegetable oil, lemon juice, and seasonings.

Mayonnaise is an interesting substance because it contains oil and vinegar, which do mix together. This is because of egg yolk. The egg yolk surrounds each fat globule and prevents it from clumping or settling out of the mayonnaise. Mayonnaise is an *emulsion:* a stable mixture of two liquids—such as oil and vinegar or lemon juice—that normally separate from each other.

Some easy-to-make salad dressings use dairy products, such as buttermilk, sour cream, or yogurt, instead of oil and vinegar or mayonnaise.

MAKING MAYONNAISE

Materials

2 egg yolks

1 teaspoon salt

1 teaspoon sugar

3 tablespoons vinegar

2 cups oil

5-quart bowl

electric mixer

Purpose

To show how oil and vinegar can be mixed together.

Procedure

1. Place egg yolks in a 5-quart mixing bowl.

2. Add salt and sugar to egg yolks and mix at medium speed until blended.

3. Mix in oil a few drops at a time at high speed until ½ cup of oil has been added. Mix in the rest of the oil about 2 tablespoons at a time. Add the vinegar as the mixture starts to thicken.

4. Cover bowl and place in refrigerator. Mayonnaise will keep for two days.

What Happened?

The mixer splits the oil droplets into smaller droplets, and the egg yolk surrounds the fat droplets so they don't clump together. Constant beating and the addition of oil in very small amounts help make and maintain small oil droplets.

Italian Dressing

Time
15 minutes

Tools
small bowl

plastic wrap

Makes
15 1-tablespoon servings

Italian dressing is oil with vinegar, lime juice,
or lemon juice that is seasoned.
This recipe uses olive oil.

Ingredients

½ cup olive oil

4 tablespoons lime juice

2 tablespoons vinegar

¼ teaspoon oregano

¼ teaspoon salt

¼ teaspoon white pepper

½ teaspoon garlic powder

¼ teaspoon sugar

1 tablespoon green pepper, finely chopped

1 teaspoon red pepper, finely chopped

1 teaspoon onion, finely chopped

• • • • • •
Before using an
oil-and-vinegar dressing,
don't forget to shake it!
• • • • • •

Steps

1. Combine the olive oil, lime juice, vinegar, oregano, salt, white pepper, garlic powder, and sugar in a small bowl.

2. Add the other ingredients and mix well.

3. Cover the bowl with plastic wrap and refrigerate. This dressing will keep for up to 7 days.

Raspberry Dressing

This dressing gets its name and distinctive flavor from raspberry vinegar. Vinegar is one of the world's oldest cooking ingredients. The best vinegars are made from wine. Vinegars may be flavored with herb or fruit flavoring such as rosemary, chili pepper, lemon, or raspberry.

Time
10 minutes

Tools
small bowl

plastic wrap

Makes
10 1-tablespoon servings

Ingredients

2 tablespoons olive oil

½ cup raspberry vinegar

1 teaspoon sugar

¼ teaspoon salt

Steps

1. Combine the olive oil, vinegar, sugar, and salt in a small bowl and mix well.

2. Cover the bowl with plastic wrap and refrigerate. This dressing will keep for up to 5 days.

•••••••••••• Thousand Island Dressing ••••••••••

Time
10 minutes

Tools
small bowl

plastic wrap

Makes
12 1-tablespoon servings

*You don't need to go to the
Thousand Islands on the St. Lawrence River
to enjoy this dressing.*

Ingredients

½ cup fat-free or low-fat
mayonnaise
or
homemade mayonnaise
(page 87)

¼ cup chili sauce

1 tablespoon sweet pickle
relish

Steps

1. Combine the mayonnaise, chili sauce, and relish in a
small bowl and mix well.

2. Cover the bowl with plastic wrap and refrigerate. This
dressing will keep for up to 3 days.

• • • • • •
*Chili sauce is a spicy
thick sauce made from
tomatoes, sweet peppers,
chili peppers, onions, and
spices. You can buy mild,
hot, or very hot chili sauce.*
• • • • • •

Russian Dressing

*Try this dressing on a sandwich
for a change of pace.*

Ingredients

1 cup fat-free or low-fat
mayonnaise
or
homemade mayonnaise
(page 87)

¼ cup chili sauce

2 tablespoons green pepper,
finely chopped

2 tablespoons onion, finely
chopped

Time
15 minutes

Tools
small bowl

cutting board

plastic wrap

Makes
24 1-tablespoon servings

Steps

1. Combine the mayonnaise and chili sauce in a small
bowl.

2. Place the green pepper and onion in the bowl with the
other ingredients and mix well.

3. Cover with plastic wrap and refrigerate. This dressing
will keep for up to 3 days.

············ Honey-Yogurt Dressing ············

Time
15 minutes

Tools
small bowl

grater

plastic wrap

Makes
20 1-tablespoon servings

• • • • •
Ground ginger *comes
from the root of the ginger
plant, which grows in
semitropical areas.*
• • • • •

*This is a great dressing to liven up
fresh fruit salads.*

Ingredients

1 cup plain low-fat or nonfat
  yogurt

2 tablespoons honey

1 tablespoon lemon juice

¼ teaspoon ground ginger

1½ tablespoons grated orange
  peel

Steps

1. Combine the yogurt, honey, lemon juice, and ginger in
a small bowl and mix well.

2. Grate the orange peel and mix it with the rest of the
ingredients.

3. Cover with plastic wrap and refrigerate. This dressing
will keep for up to 7 days.

Tuny Salad

Tuny Salad can be used as a sandwich filling, on crackers, or even in an ice cream cone. Add cooked macaroni to it and you'll have Macaroni and Tuna Salad, a great main dish for lunch or supper—just top with fresh vegetables like cherry tomatoes.

Time
10 minutes

Tools
medium bowl

knife

cutting board

Makes
2 servings

Ingredients

1 can (6½ oz.) tuna fish, packed in water

1 small dill or sweet pickle

3 tablespoons fat-free or low-fat mayonnaise
    or

homemade mayonnaise (page 87)

1 tablespoon vinegar

2 tablespoons seasoned bread crumbs

Steps

1. Open tuna fish can and drain off the liquid. Put the tuna fish in a medium bowl.

2. Using a knife on a cutting board, chop the pickle and place in the bowl with the tuna fish.

3. Add mayonnaise, vinegar, and bread crumbs to the tuna fish and mix well.

4. Serve immediately on bread or crackers, or cover with plastic wrap and refrigerate. The salad will keep for up to 2 days.

Waldorf Salad

Time
20 minutes

Tools
knife

cutting board

medium bowl

Makes
2 servings

Waldorf Salad, a mixture of chopped apples, celery, and walnuts, got its name from the Waldorf-Astoria Hotel in New York City, where it was first made. Mayonnaise is used to hold it together. It is usually served as a side dish on a lettuce leaf.

Ingredients

1 large red apple

2 stalks celery

2 tablespoons raisins

1 teaspoon chopped nuts

2 tablespoons fat-free or low-fat mayonnaise

lettuce leaves

Steps

1. Wash the apple. Using a knife on a cutting board, cut it in half and remove the seeds. Cut into ½-inch cubes.

2. Remove any celery leaves and wash the celery. Slice the celery into ¼-inch slices.

3. Combine apple, celery, raisins, nuts, and mayonnaise in a medium bowl. Mix well.

4. Serve immediately on lettuce leaves or cover with plastic wrap and refrigerate. The salad will keep for up to 3 days.

• • • • • Three-Bean Salad • • • • •

Three-Bean Salad is a collection of three different kinds of beans in an oil-and-vinegar dressing. The beans are usually green beans, wax beans, and kidney beans, but you could use any cooked bean or partially cooked vegetable instead.

Ingredients

14-oz. can kidney beans

15-oz. can green beans

15-oz. can wax beans

1 medium onion

⅓ cup vinegar

2 tablespoons vegetable oil

¼ teaspoon salt

⅛ teaspoon pepper

Steps

1. Open the cans of kidney beans, green beans, and wax beans.

2. Empty the cans into a colander to drain the liquid.

3. Remove the outer skin of the onion. Using a knife on a cutting board, cut the onion in half and chop.

4. Combine the vinegar, oil, salt, and pepper in a small bowl.

5. Put the three kinds of beans and the chopped onion into a medium bowl. Pour the oil and vinegar dressing over the beans.

6. Cover with plastic wrap and refrigerate for 2 hours before serving. This salad will keep for up to 7 days.

Time
20 minutes to prepare
plus
2 hours to refrigerate

Tools
colander

knife

cutting board

small bowl

medium bowl

plastic wrap

Makes
8 servings

• • • • •

Kidney beans are large, kidney-shaped beans. They are available red or white, but red is much more common. They are a favorite in Mexican and Italian cooking.

• • • • •

CHAPTER 11

MAKE-YOUR-OWN PASTA SAUCES

Many of the foods we eat, such as tomato sauce or spaghetti sauce, are flavored and seasoned to make them taste good. Salt, sugar, and pepper are commonly used to improve the flavor of foods. Salt is a chemical compound made of sodium and chloride. It is found in nature as underground and surface deposits of rock salt and can also come from evaporated seawater (sea salt). Americans like salt—we each eat an average of close to a tablespoon a day, most of which comes from processed foods.

Herbs and spices are also used to flavor foods. Herbs and spices differ only in that herbs are leaves and stems of plants, and spices come

from other parts of plants such as the bark, root, or seeds. Spices are almost always dried, whereas many herbs can be bought fresh at the supermarket or grown at home. Professional cooks prefer fresh herbs to dried. Fresh herbs are less concentrated than dried herbs. Herbs can also be used as alternatives to salt for flavoring foods.

HERBS

First, let's take a look at five popular herbs.

Basil is a leaf and a member of the mint family. In ancient Greece, basil was the herb of kings. It was the symbol of love in some cultures and the symbol of hate in others. Today, basil is known as the "tomato herb" because it gives tomatoes an excellent flavor.

It is used to season vegetables, especially tomatoes, eggplant, zucchini, squash, carrots, and cabbage. Basil also can be added to soups, stews, and spaghetti sauce.

Basil

Dill is available either as crushed leaves (called *dill weed*) or as the whole seed. They both have the familiar "dill pickle" flavor, although the seed is more flavorful than the leaves. Dill was brought to America by the Germans, Scots, and Irish.

Dill is used to season vegetables such as green beans, potatoes, carrots, and broccoli, and in cold salads such as potato salad and cucumber salad.

Dill

Oregano was known and used by the ancient Greeks and Romans. It was almost unknown in the United States until after World War II, when the servicemen stationed in Italy brought back a taste for Italian dishes containing oregano. Today oregano, with its pungent, spicy flavor, is one of the most popular herbs in this country.

Oregano is used to flavor tomato sauce, spaghetti sauce, pizzas, and other Italian dishes. It can also be used to flavor meat, poultry, tomatoes, eggplant, zucchini, peas, squash, and herb bread.

Oregano

Parsley is the most widely used herb. Its green curly or flat leaves have a slightly sweet flavor. Sprigs of parsley are commonly used on almost any food as a garnish, or decoration.

Tarragon's name comes from the French word *estragon*, which means "little dragon". There is nothing dangerous about this herb, but it is a bit strong in flavor.

Parsley

Tarragon leaves can be used in salads, salad dressings, poultry and fish dishes, and with vegetables such as peas and tomatoes. It is also used in sauces.

Tarragon

SPICES

Now let's take a look at some spices that, because of their sweetness, are popular in baking.

Allspice is a small brown berry that originated in the West Indies and Latin America. Its flavor is like a blend of cinnamon, cloves, and nutmeg.

Cinnamon is from the bark of cinnamon or cassia trees. Cinnamon sticks are the dried-out bark that has curled up.

Cloves and **nutmeg** are from Indonesia. Cloves are the dried unopened flower buds of a tropical tree, and nutmeg is the seed of the fruit of the nutmeg tree. Both of these spices are used with fruits. Nutmeg also works well with certain vegetables, such as potatoes and squash.

EXPERIMENT

GROWING YOUR OWN SWEET BASIL PLANT

Purpose

To grow a tasty herb.

Materials

4 bush basil seeds
6-inch flowerpot and potting soil

Procedure

1. Plant seeds ¼ inch deep and 4 inches apart in potting soil in flower pot.

2. Water thoroughly and place in shade until seedlings appear, within about 2 weeks.

3. Put plants in full sun or partial shade. Keep soil lightly moist. Bush basil will grow about 10 inches tall in 6 to 8 weeks. Pinch off and use leaves as soon as you like—they will grow back quickly.

What Happened?

Bush basil is an excellent variety of basil to grow indoors because the plant is fairly small. Sweet basil normally grows to be 2 to 3 feet tall. Use the fresh basil leaves in recipes to provide a pleasant, spicy flavor. Fresh basil leaves can also be wrapped in aluminum foil and frozen for up to 6 months.

Tomato Sauce

*Make this old favorite without opening a can!
It's not hard!*

Ingredients

6 medium fresh tomatoes

1 medium onion

vegetable oil cooking spray

½ teaspoon sugar

½ teaspoon dried basil leaves
or
2 teaspoons fresh basil leaves

¼ teaspoon garlic powder

Steps

1. Heat at least 5 inches of water in saucepan until it boils. Plunge tomatoes into boiling water for 30 seconds. Be careful not to let the water splash you.

2. Remove the tomatoes with a large spoon and put them in a colander. Rinse in cold water. Remove the skins with your hands or a paring knife on a cutting board. Chop the tomatoes into small pieces.

3. Remove the outer skin of the onion. Using a knife on a cutting board, cut the onion in half and chop.

4. Spray a large frying pan with cooking spray. Heat the frying pan over medium heat for 1 minute.

5. Sauté the onion in the frying pan for 3 to 4 minutes.

6. Add tomatoes and sugar, basil, and garlic powder to the frying pan.

7. Simmer for 15 to 20 minutes to cook and blend flavors. Be careful not to overcook.

8. Serve over cooked pasta.

Variation

Meat Sauce Brown ½ pound lean ground beef, chicken, or turkey in step 5 with onion. Drain any fat before going on to the next step.

Time
30 to 40 minutes

Tools
medium saucepan

colander

paring knife

knife

cutting board

large frying pan

Makes
8 ½-cup servings

• • • • •
*Plunging tomatoes
in hot water makes
them easier to peel.*
• • • • •

····Primavera Sauce····

Time
20 minutes

Tools
steamer basket

saucepan with lid

large frying pan

Makes
6 ½-cup servings

• • • • •
If you don't want to use the frozen vegetables in this recipe, you can use any fresh vegetables you like.
• • • • •

Primavera is an Italian word that means "spring." For this dish, it means any spring vegetables can be included.

Ingredients

1 10-oz. bag frozen Italian-style vegetables

vegetable oil cooking spray

1 cup evaporated skim milk

¼ teaspoon dill weed

¼ teaspoon oregano

¼ teaspoon basil

¼ teaspoon salt

¼ teaspoon pepper

Steps

1. Set up the steamer basket in a saucepan and add water just up to the bottom of the basket. Turn the heat to high.

2. When the water starts to boil, add the frozen vegetables. Put the lid on and cook vegetables for 5 minutes.

3. Spray a large frying pan with cooking spray. Heat the frying pan over medium heat for 1 minute.

4. Spoon steamed vegetables into frying pan. Sauté until they are tender but still crisp, about 5 minutes.

5. Add evaporated skim milk and dill, oregano, basil, salt, and pepper. Simmer on low heat for 3 to 5 minutes, until warm.

6. Serve over cooked pasta.

Blender Pesto Sauce

The dominant ingredient in pesto sauce is basil.
Use the basil leaves you've grown in this recipe.
Pesto sauce is popular on hot pasta.

Time
15 minutes

Tools
blender

Makes
4 ½-cup servings

Ingredients

1½ cups firmly packed basil leaves

¼ cup grated parmesan cheese

¼ cup pine nuts

1 clove garlic

½ cup olive oil

¼ cup pine nuts

Steps

1. Wash basil leaves and pat dry.

2. In a blender combine basil, cheese, pine nuts, garlic, and olive oil.

3. Blend at medium speed until mixture is smooth.

4. Add 1 tablespoon hot water to blender and blend at medium for 1 minute.

5. Serve sauce on hot pasta. Sprinkle with remaining cheese and pine nuts.

• • • • •

Pine nuts *are small seeds*
from one of several
pine tree varieties. They
have a sweet, faint pine
flavor. Other names for
pine nuts include
pignolia *and* ***piñon.***

• • • • •

CHAPTER 12
MAKE-YOUR-OWN CHEESE

You may already know that cheese is made from milk, but have you ever wondered how? In the experiment in this chapter you are going to make your own cottage cheese. Cottage cheese is the result of a chemical reaction that occurs when the **protein** in the milk is mixed with an acid. The protein becomes firm, or **coagulates**. This coagulated protein is called *curds*.

Cottage cheese is a soft, moist white cheese with a mild flavor. It was made in home kitchens all over Europe for centuries and was called "cottage" cheese because farmers made the cheese in their own cottages. Cottage cheese is made from skim milk, which has almost no fat. One cup provides as much protein as an average serving of meat, poultry, or fish. Some of the cottage cheese available at the supermarket has cream added to it to make it creamier and richer.

In addition to being eaten plain, cottage cheese is popular in cheese dishes, such as lasagne, and with fruit as a light lunch or dessert.

MAKING CURDS AND WHEY

Materials

1 quart skim milk

medium saucepan

2 tablespoons lemon juice

long-handled wooden spoon

cheesecloth (Cheesecloth is a soft fabric made of cotton that allows liquids to go through it but holds on to solids. It looks like bandage gauze.)

colander

measuring cup and spoons

Purpose

To show how cottage cheese is made and how protein coagulates.

Procedure

1. Pour the milk into a medium saucepan.

2. Bring the milk to a boil using medium-high heat. Watch for bubbles; this means the milk is starting to boil.

3. While the milk is heating, measure two tablespoons of lemon juice into a small cup.

4. Once the milk boils, remove the pan from the burner and mix in the lemon juice using the wooden spoon.

5. Return the pan to the burner and mix until you see curds separating from the liquid. Turn off the heat, remove the pan from the burner, and let it cool for a few minutes.

6. Meanwhile, line a colander with cheesecloth and place the colander in the sink. Pour the milk into the colander. The curds should collect in the cheesecloth.

7. Once all the liquid has drained, remove the curds from the cheesecloth and place in a bowl. This is cottage cheese.

What Happened?

The addition of lemon juice, which is an acid, creates a small storm in the milk that results in the formation of *curds*, white lumps about the consistency of custard, and *whey*, a thin, cloudy liquid.

Fruited Parfaits

Time
10 minutes

Tools
small mixing bowl

spoon

4 serving bowls or parfait glasses

Makes
4 1-cup servings

• • • • •
Did you know that it takes more than 3 quarts of milk to make 1 pound of cottage cheese?
• • • • •

This is great for parties.

Ingredients

1 cup cottage cheese

1 cup plain nonfat yogurt

1 cup dry breakfast cereal (pick a crunchy one)

1 cup fruit, fresh or canned

maple syrup
or
honey

Steps

1. Mix the cottage cheese and yogurt in a small mixing bowl.

2. Spoon a layer of cereal into the bottom of 4 serving bowls or parfait glasses, using all the cereal.

3. Spoon a layer of the yogurt–cottage cheese mixture into each of the bowls, using it all.

4. Spoon a layer of fruit on top of each parfait. Top with maple syrup or honey. Serve.

THE REST OF THE CHEESE STORY

Now that you have made cottage cheese, you may be wondering how other cheeses are made. There are many variations in the cheese-making process that produce the wide variety of cheeses you see at the grocery store. Cheese can be made from the milk of different animals, and the type of milk gives each variety of cheese its own special flavor. Milk from cows, goats, and sheep is most commonly used to make cheese.

Most cheese is not ready to eat until it has had time to ripen, or age. During this time, the flavor of the cheese develops. Cottage cheese does not go through a ripening process. Other unripened cheeses include ricotta cheese, cream cheese, and mozzarella (the cheese most often used on pizzas).

Ripening is brought about by certain bacteria or molds that give each cheese a distinctive taste. These are not harmful bacteria or molds. Mold is a natural part of certain cheeses such as blue cheese. In blue cheese, the mold is easy to see because it is blue. In other ripened cheeses, such as cheddar or Swiss, the bacteria or mold is added by the cheesemaker and is invisible.

American cheese is actually a combination of cheddar and other cheeses along with special ingredients that make it stay fresh for a long time. Called a *process cheese*, American cheese is noted for its mild flavor and its ability to melt nicely on a cheeseburger or in a grilled cheese sandwich.

The All-American Cheeseburger

Time
15 minutes to prepare
plus
20 to 25 minutes to cook

Tools
knife

cutting board

large mixing bowl

wooden spoon

roasting pan with rack

Makes
4 cheeseburgers

• • • • •
Worcestershire sauce
is a thin, dark-brown
sauce used to season
meats, gravies, and soups.
• • • • •

Did you know that most hamburgers sold are cheeseburgers? Here's a great recipe to make at home.

Ingredients

1 medium onion

1 pound lean ground beef

1 tablespoon Worcestershire sauce

½ teaspoon garlic powder

4 slices American cheese

4 hamburger buns

Steps

1. Preheat the oven to 350°F.

2. Remove the outer skin of the onion. Using a knife on a cutting board, slice the onion in half, then cut each half into three pieces. Chop onion.

3. In a large mixing bowl, combine the onion, ground beef, Worcestershire sauce, and garlic powder with a wooden spoon.

4. Shape the meat into four burgers.

5. Place burgers on a rack in a roasting pan and bake for 15 minutes at 350°F.

6. Remove the burgers from the oven and place 1 slice of cheese on each burger.

7. Return the burgers to the oven for approximately 5 minutes for medium burgers and for approximately 10 minutes for well-done burgers.

8. Serve on hamburger buns with your favorite toppings.

CHAPTER 13

AKE-YOUR-OWN WHIPPED CREAM AND BUTTER

Whipped cream is a popular topping for many desserts, such as ice-cream sundaes, fruit, and pies. The best whipped cream is made from heavy cream. Heavy cream is made from the fatty part of fresh milk. Regular milk and light cream will not whip well, because they don't contain enough fat.

As you whip heavy cream, you trap air in the cream in the form of tiny bubbles. These air bubbles make whipped cream light. The nonfat, watery part of the cream that encloses the air bubbles is supported by the fat. The more fat in your cream, the more easily the bubbles will be supported.

It takes only a few minutes to whip cream. Make sure the whipping cream is very cold. The whipping bowl and beaters should also be chilled. If you whip the cream too long, it will change into butter right before your eyes. You'll know you have gone too far if you see small lumps in the liquid. These lumps are butter. Butter is formed because too much agitation (mixing) warms the cream to the point that the air bubbles are broken and liquid fat starts to stick together. This liquid fat is butter.

Butter has always been made by a process like whipping that is called *churning*. To churn butter at home, put whipping cream into a large jar and shake the jar for 20 minutes. Shaking forces the fat droplets to stick together and form butter. The butter droplets grow larger and result in a semisolid mass of butter and a liquid. The liquid left over from churning butter is called *buttermilk*.

Butter is used to make buttercream frosting for icing cakes. Buttercream icings are light, smooth mixtures of butter (or margarine) and sugar.

EXPERIMENT • MAKING WHIPPED CREAM FROM LIGHT CREAM AND HEAVY CREAM

Purpose

To determine how fat content affects the whipping of cream.

Materials

1 cup heavy cream
1 cup light cream
2-quart mixing bowl
electric mixer

Procedure

1. Using the heavy cream, make Homemade Whipped Cream (next page).

2. Using the light cream, make Homemade Whipped Cream (wash your equipment first).

3. Which type of cream produced more whipped cream?

What Happened?

Heavy cream contains more fat than light cream. When you whip heavy cream, it produces more whipped cream than does light cream. This occurs because the fat helps support the air bubbles that are created during whipping.

Homemade Whipped Cream

*Here's a recipe for basic whipped cream.
To flavor whipped cream,
try one of the five variations.*

Ingredients

1 cup heavy cream

Steps

1. Put the mixing bowl and the beaters from the electric mixer in the freezer for 20 minutes.

2. Remove the bowl from the freezer and put the heavy cream into it.

3. With an electric mixer on high speed, beat until stiff peaks form when beaters are lifted. This takes about 2 to 3 minutes. Do not overbeat!

Variations

Add any one of the following ingredients to the cream when soft peaks begin to form while whipping. Continue to beat until stiff peaks form when the beaters are lifted.

- 1 tablespoon confectioners' sugar
- 1 teaspoon lemon extract
- 1 teaspoon vanilla extract
- 1 teaspoon sugar plus ¼ teaspoon cinnamon
- 1 teaspoon sugar plus ¼ teaspoon nutmeg

Time
10 minutes

Tools
2-quart mixing bowl

electric mixer

Makes
8 ¼-cup servings

Frozen Yogurt Sundae

Now that you've made whipped cream, you may want to make sundaes to go with it. Simply place one scoop of your favorite frozen yogurt in a sundae dish and top with whipped cream. Then choose any of these healthy toppings.

- freshly sliced strawberries or bananas
- sliced kiwis or melon cubes
- canned fruit, such as crushed pineapple
- dried fruit, such as raisins
- your favorite cold cereal
- crushed chocolate graham crackers (or other cookie)
- wheat germ
- chopped nuts
- warm applesauce

Homemade Buttercream Frosting

Buttercream frosting uses butter and confectioners' sugar to make a delicious cake icing. Make sure you refrigerate it, because it contains butter and a little milk.

Time
10 minutes

Tools
medium bowl

electric mixer

Makes
2 cups (enough to frost a
9-inch 2-layer cake
or
24 cupcakes)

Ingredients

½ cup butter

½ pound confectioners' sugar

½ teaspoon salt

½ teaspoon vanilla extract

3 tablespoons skim or low-fat milk, plus additional tablespoon if needed

½ pound confectioners' sugar

Steps

1. Put the butter, ½ pound confectioners' sugar, salt, and vanilla extract into a medium bowl.

2. Beat with an electric mixer until creamy.

3. Add milk and the remaining ½ pound confectioners' sugar and beat 1 to 2 minutes on medium speed until creamy. If too thick, add 1 more tablespoon milk.

• • • • •
Confectioners' sugar
is table sugar that has been ground to a fine powder.
• • • • •

•••• Basic Cupcakes ••••

Time
20 minutes to prepare
plus
20 to 25 minutes to bake

Tools
muffin pan

large bowl

medium bowl

wooden spoon

spoon

Makes
12 cupcakes

• • • • •

*Don't ice any cake
while it is warm, or the
cake will stick to your
spreader and the icing
will get loose and runny.*

• • • • •

*Ice these cupcakes with
Homemade Buttercream Frosting.*

Ingredients

1 tablespoon shortening	1 egg
1¼ cups all-purpose flour	¾ cup skim or low-fat milk
1 cup sugar	⅓ cup melted shortening
1½ teaspoons baking powder	1 teaspoon vanilla extract
½ teaspoon salt	

Steps

1. Preheat oven to 400°F.

2. Grease bottoms and sides of muffin cups with shortening, or use a nonstick muffin pan, or line muffin pan with paper cupcake cups.

3. Mix the flour, sugar, baking powder, and salt in a large bowl.

4. Mix the egg, milk, melted shortening, and vanilla extract in medium bowl.

5. Add milk mixture all at once to the large bowl with the flour mixture.

6. Mix ingredients with wooden spoon until well blended.

7. Using a large spoon, fill each muffin cup two-thirds full with batter.

8. Bake for 20 to 25 minutes at 400°F or until golden brown.

9. Using oven mitts, remove the pan from the oven and let cool for 15 minutes on a cooling rack.

10. Remove cupcakes from the pan and let cool 1 hour.

11. Ice the cupcakes using a sandwich spreader and Homemade Buttercream Frosting. Dip the sandwich spreader into hot water for a few minutes before icing the cupcakes. A warm spreader will spread the icing faster and more easily.

CHAPTER 14

MAKE-YOUR-OWN PUDDING MIX

Puddings are creamy desserts made from milk, sugar, a thickener such as cornstarch, and flavorings. Cornstarch is a white, powdery substance that comes from corn. Pudding mixes are readily available, but you can make your own in 15 minutes or less. The Homemade Pudding Mix in this chapter can be used to make many different puddings and pudding sundaes.

USING CORNSTARCH TO THICKEN

Purpose

To show that cornstarch will thicken a sauce.

Materials

2 8-ounce cans tomato sauce

1 tablespoon cornstarch

3 tablespoons water

2 small saucepans

measuring cup

wooden spoon

Procedure

1. Put 1 can of tomato sauce into each saucepan and put each on medium heat. Heat for 3 minutes.

2. Put the water into the measuring cup, add the cornstarch, and mix well.

3. Add the cornstarch mixture to the first saucepan, and increase to high heat. Stir constantly for 2 minutes.

4. Reduce the heat of the tomato sauce–cornstarch mixture to medium and stir for 4 minutes.

5. What did the tomato sauce look like in each pan at the end? Which sauce thickened?

What Happened?

Cornstarch is the starch from kernels of corn. Starch is a form of carbohydrate that does not dissolve in water at room temperature. However, as water is heated, cornstarch granules absorb water and swell up to many times their original size. The result is a liquid that is thicker. Because cornstarch absorbs water, it can be used to thicken sauces, soups, and other foods.

Homemade Pudding Mix

This mix is a snap to make. Once it's done, you can use it to make many different puddings.

Time
15 minutes

Tools
2 large bowls

sifter

Makes
5 cups

Ingredients

3½ cups powdered milk   ¾ cup cornstarch

1 cup sugar

Steps

1. Mix together the powdered milk, sugar, and cornstarch in a large bowl.

2. Put the sifter in another large bowl and scoop the powdered milk mixture into the sifter.

3. Sift all the powdered milk mixture into the bowl.

4. Cover tightly and store in a cool, dark place. The mix will keep for 1 month.

Nilla Vanilla Pudding

Time
20 minutes
plus
1 ¼ hours cooling time

Tools
saucepan

whip

bowl
or
serving dishes

Makes
6 ½-cup servings

You can dress up this pudding by topping it with whipped cream and a wafer cookie.

Ingredients

1 cup Homemade Pudding Mix

1¾ cups hot water

2 tablespoons margarine

1 teaspoon vanilla extract

Steps

1. Combine the pudding mix and water in a saucepan and stir until the pudding mix is dissolved.

2. Put the saucepan on a burner and turn to medium heat. Bring pudding to a boil (look for bubbles, which mean that it's starting to boil).

3. Reduce the heat to low, and gently simmer about 2 minutes, stirring vigorously.

4. Remove the pan from the heat and whisk in the margarine and vanilla extract.

5. Carefully pour the pudding into a bowl or serving dishes. Let stand 15 minutes, then chill for 1 hour before serving.

The Richest Chocolate Pudding

If you love chocolate,
this is the only pudding for you.

Ingredients

1¾ cups hot water

2 squares unsweetened chocolate

1 cup Homemade Pudding Mix

2 tablespoons margarine

1 teaspoon vanilla extract

Steps

1. Put the hot water into a 2-cup measuring cup and add chocolate squares so that they melt.

2. Put the pudding mix in a small saucepan. Add the melted chocolate and water and stir until the pudding mix is dissolved.

3. Put the saucepan on a burner and turn to medium heat. Bring the pudding to a boil (look for bubbles, which mean that it's starting to boil).

4. Reduce the heat to low and gently simmer about 2 minutes, stirring vigorously.

5. Remove the pan from the heat and whisk in the margarine and vanilla extract.

6. Carefully pour the pudding into a bowl or serving dishes. Let stand 15 minutes, then chill for 1 hour before serving.

Time
20 minutes
plus
1¼ hours cooling time

Tools
2-cup measuring cup

small saucepan

whip

bowl
or
serving dishes

Makes
6 ½-cup servings

• • • • •
Unsweetened chocolate
is pure chocolate without
any added sugar.
It may also be called
baking chocolate.
Because of its bitter flavor,
it is used mostly in
cooking or baking when a
sweetener will be added.
• • • • •

••••• Rich Caramel Pudding •••••

Time
20 minutes
plus
1¼ hours cooling time

Tools
saucepan

whip

bowl
or
serving dishes

Makes
6 ½-cup servings

*This pudding uses caramel candies
to get its rich flavor.*

Ingredients

1 cup Homemade Pudding Mix

1¾ cups hot water

8 to 10 caramel candy pieces

2 tablespoons margarine

1 teaspoon vanilla extract

Steps

1. Combine the pudding mix and hot water in the saucepan and stir until the pudding mix is dissolved.

2. Add caramel candies to the saucepan.

3. Put the saucepan on a burner and turn to medium heat. Bring pudding to a boil (look for bubbles, which mean that it's starting to boil).

4. Reduce the heat to low and gently simmer about 2 minutes, stirring vigorously.

5. Remove the pan from the heat and whisk in the margarine and vanilla extract.

6. Carefully pour the pudding into a bowl or serving dishes. Let stand 15 minutes, then chill for 1 hour before serving.

···· Fruit 'n Pudding Sundae ····

This is a great idea for parties. You can substitute any fruit you like for the ones we've suggested.

Ingredients

1 recipe Nilla Vanilla Pudding (page 116)

½ cup heavy cream

2 bananas

1 kiwi

½ cup strawberries (fresh *or* frozen and thawed)

sprinkles (jimmies)

6 maraschino cherries

Steps

1. Follow directions for Nilla Vanilla Pudding and refrigerate for at least one hour.

2. Put a medium bowl into the freezer for 10 minutes.

3. Remove the bowl from the freezer and pour the heavy cream into the bowl.

4. Whip the heavy cream with an electric mixer on high speed until stiff peaks form when the beaters are lifted. Do not overbeat!

5. Peel the bananas and the kiwi. Using a knife on a cutting board, slice strawberries, banana, and kiwi.

6. To make sundaes, split half of the fruit between the 6 sundae cups.

7. Top with pudding, then whipped cream, more fruit, sprinkles, and cherries.

Time
20 minutes
plus
1¼ hours cooling time

Tools
medium bowl

electric mixer

knife

cutting board

6 sundae cups

Makes
6 sundaes

CHAPTER 15

MAKE-YOUR-OWN ICE POPS

Everyone knows that ice pops are made of ice, but have you ever thought about what ice really is? Ice is a solid, one of three states of matter. Ice has weight and it takes up space. Ice also has a shape of its own. When ice melts, it changes to water, a liquid. Liquids are another state of matter. Liquids also have weight and take up space, but they don't have a shape of their own. When water boils, it changes to steam, a gas (the last state of matter). It still has weight and takes up space, but it has no shape.

Ice has some unique properties. When you put an ice cube tray full of water into the freezer, the water expands (gets bigger) during freezing. Most substances contract (get smaller) when frozen. Ice is also less dense than water, so ice cubes float.

FREEZING WATER

Materials

½ cup water

paper cup

pen or pencil

Purpose:

To observe that water expands during freezing.

Procedure

1. Pour the water into the paper cup.

2. Using a pen or pencil, mark how high the water is on the inside of the cup.

3. Put the cup of water in the freezer for 4 hours.

4. Open the freezer and take out the cup. Where is the top of the cube of ice in relation to the line you drew?

What Happened?

As ice crystals start to form in the water, the water expands by about one-eleventh. This expansion causes the top of the ice cube to be higher than the line drawn. The same process occurs when food is packed into freezer containers without extra space for expansion.

Fruisicles

This recipe is for basic frozen-fruit-juice-on-a-stick. Any fruit juice will do!

Time
10 minutes
plus
2 hours freezing time

Tools
six 3-ounce paper cups
and 6 wooden sticks
or
plastic ice-pop molds

aluminum foil

Makes
6 pops

Ingredients

2¼ cups of your favorite juice

Steps

1. Pour the juice into 3-ounce paper cups or plastic molds.

2. Cover each cup with a small piece of aluminum foil and put them in the freezer until the juice is thick and slushy, about 20 to 40 minutes.

3. Remove the cups from the freezer. Insert a wooden stick through the middle of the foil covering each cup and push to the bottom of the cup. If using plastic molds, insert plastic stick.

4. Return the cups to the freezer.

5. Freeze until the juice is completely hard. To eat, hold onto the stick and peel off the paper cup, or hold the plastic mold under hot tap water to loosen the pop.

Variation

Fruited Pops   Add small chunks of fresh or canned fruit to the juice, such as crushed pineapple, mashed bananas, or chopped peaches. Use ½ to 1 cup of fruit for every 2¼ cups of juice.

Yogurt Fruisicles

If you like a creamier popsicle, try these.

Ingredients

½ cup frozen juice   1¾ cups plain low-fat or nonfat yogurt

Steps

1. Mix juice concentrate and plain yogurt in a small bowl.

2. Pour the juice-yogurt mixture into the 3-ounce paper cups or plastic molds.

3. Cover each cup with a small piece of aluminum foil and put the cups into the freezer until the mixture is thick and slushy, about 20 to 40 minutes.

4. Remove the cups from the freezer. Insert a wooden stick through the foil covering each cup and push to the bottom of the cup. If using plastic molds, insert plastic stick.

5. Return the cups to the freezer.

6. Freeze until the juice is completely hard. To eat, hold onto the stick and peel off the paper cup, or hold the plastic mold under hot tap water to loosen the pop.

Time
10 minutes
plus
2 hours freezing time

Tools
small bowl

six 3-ounce paper cups and
wooden sticks
or
plastic ice-pop molds

aluminum foil

Makes
6 pops

• • • • •
*If you want more
sweetness, use more juice
concentrate. If you want
more creaminess,
use more yogurt.*
• • • • •

Pudding Pops

Time
10 minutes
plus
2 hours freezing time

Tools
medium mixing bowl

electric mixer

six 3-ounce paper cups
and wooden sticks
or
plastic ice-pops molds

aluminum foil

Makes
6 pops

For a vanilla-and-chocolate pop, make both vanilla and chocolate puddings and pour equal amounts into each cup. For a marbled effect, move the blade of a table knife around the cup.

Ingredients

Instant pudding mix, any
flavor, small box
or
Homemade Pudding Mix (page 115)

skim or low-fat milk

Steps

1. Prepare pudding with milk according to package directions, or make Homemade Pudding Mix.

2. Pour the pudding into the 3-ounce paper cups or plastic molds.

3. Cover each cup with a small piece of aluminum foil and put them into the freezer for 15 minutes.

4. Remove the cups from freezer. Insert a wooden stick through the foil covering each cup and push to the bottom of the cup. If using plastic molds, insert plastic stick.

5. Return the cups to the freezer.

6. Freeze until the pudding is completely hard. To eat, hold onto the stick and peel off the paper cup, or hold the plastic mold under hot tap water to loosen the pop.

PART 3

SCIENCE IN THE SUPERMARKET

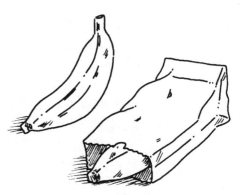

CHAPTER 16

RIPE OR NOT RIPE?

When you're at the supermarket, have you ever wondered why shoppers squeeze tomatoes, press cantaloupes, and check the color of bananas? These are all ways to check if fruit is ripe for eating, or, in other words, to see if the fruit is going to be sweet and juicy. Some fruits don't ripen after being picked. They are ripe when you buy them—these include apples, berries, citrus fruit, and grapes.

It is generally best to store these fruits in the refrigerator so they don't overripen and decay.

Among fruits that benefit from further ripening are bananas, kiwi, melon, peaches, and nectarines. As fruits ripen, they let off a gas called *ethylene gas*. Ethylene is a colorless, odorless gas that promotes ripening in most fresh fruits and vegetables. You can actually speed up the ripening process by placing fruit in a paper bag so that the ethylene gas is trapped.

The old saying about the bad apple spoiling the whole bunch is true. Damaged apples emit even more ethylene gas than undamaged ones. A damaged apple will therefore speed up the decay of any fruit stored with it.

Here's how to tell when certain fruits are ripe.

- **bananas**   A yellow banana flecked with brown spots is ripe. If the banana is green, it is not yet ripe.

- **cantaloupe** If it smells real cantaloupy, it's ripe! Also, the blossom end should feel a bit soft when you press it.

- **peaches and nectarines** When these fruits are ripe, they feel soft to the touch.

- **pineapple** The key to determining ripeness is to smell the pineapple—the more fragrant, the more ripe it is.

Let's check out some fun fruit facts! Did you know that:

- Although tomatoes are legally considered vegetables, they actually fit the definition of a fruit. Fruits are the seed-bearing part of a flowering plant. Tomatoes are filled with seeds, so they are technically a fruit. They are a little sweet like fruits, but we use them in salads and other dishes where we wouldn't think of using other fruits.

- The silvery "frost" that appears on grapes, plums, and blueberries is not dirt or a sign of damage. In fact, it is a protective coating grown by the fruit and often indicates freshness.

- You should wash berries, plums, and grapes just before eating. If these fruits are washed before storing, mold will often appear.

- The most popular fruits are (in this order) bananas, apples, and watermelon.

RIPENING BANANAS · EXPERIMENT

Materials

2 bananas with similar coloring

paper or plastic bag

Procedure

1. Put one banana on the kitchen counter, and place the other banana in a paper or plastic bag with a few small holes poked in it.

2. Write down the color of each banana every morning for 3 days, such as "half green," "all yellow," or "one-quarter black."

3. Which banana ripened (and turned black) quicker?

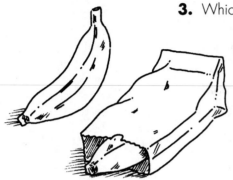

What Happened?

The banana in the paper or plastic bag ripened faster, because the ethylene gas the banana gives off is trapped in the bag, which then quickens ripening.

Dips & Spreads for Fruits & Veggies

Try these out on your favorite cut-up fruits and vegetables.

- ½ cup peanut butter with 2 tablespoons honey mixed in
- apple butter
- fruit spreads (you can mix in wheat germ)
- nonfat sour cream mixed with raisins and brown sugar
- flavored yogurts
- cottage cheese (you can mix in fruit and/or nuts)
- cheese spread
- tuna fish salad

Watermelon Butterfly Salad

This salad is fun to make and almost too pretty to eat.

Ingredients

1 slice watermelon
lettuce leaf
1 carrot, peeled

3 strawberries
4 raisins

Time
15 minutes

Tools
cutting board

knife

toothpicks

Makes
1 serving

Steps

1. Using a knife on a cutting board, cut a watermelon slice in half. On each half, cut off a small piece at the corner, forming wings.

2. Place a lettuce leaf on a plate.

3. Lay the watermelon slices on the leaf so that they look like butterfly wings. Place a carrot in the center to form the butterfly's body.

4. Using a knife on a cutting board, slice the strawberries in half. Place the slices on the watermelon to decorate the wings.

5. Insert toothpicks through raisins and place 2 on the carrot for eyes and 2 on top of the carrot for antennae.

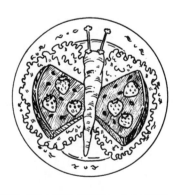

Baked Apples

Time
10 minutes to prepare
plus
45 to 60 minutes to bake

Tools
cutting board

apple corer

small bowl

baking pan

spoon

Makes
6 servings

• • • •

Some apple varieties that are good for eating fresh or baking are Golden Delicious, Granny Smith, and Rome Beauty.

• • • •

Baked apples are an easy-to-make dessert that you can make any time of the year.

Ingredients

6 apples

¼ cup brown sugar

1 teaspoon cinnamon

¼ teaspoon nutmeg

1 tablespoon vegetable oil

⅓ cup raisins

Steps

1. Preheat the oven to 375°F.

2. On a cutting board, remove cores from apples using an apple corer.

3. Put the apples in the baking pan so they stand upright.

4. In a small bowl, mix the brown sugar, cinnamon, nutmeg, vegetable oil, and raisins.

5. Fill the center of the apples with the sugar and spice mixture. Pour 1 cup water around apples.

6. Bake for 45 to 60 minutes at 375°F or until soft. Using a spoon, pour the liquid from the bottom of the pan over the apples to keep them moist. Be careful not to touch the hot pan.

Variation

Baked Pears   Substitute 6 pears for apples. Bake for 45 to 60 minutes or until tender.

Baked Peaches   Substitute 6 peaches for apples. Slice in half and remove pit. Bake for 20 to 25 minutes or until tender.

Apple cobbler is as tasty as apple pie, but it doesn't contain as much fat.

Ingredients

vegetable oil cooking spray

6 Granny Smith or Macintosh apples

2 tablespoons lemon juice

1 tablespoon whole-wheat flour

1½ teaspoons cinnamon

3 tablespoons margarine

½ cup whole-wheat flour

1 cup old-fashioned oats

½ teaspoon cinnamon

¼ teaspoon nutmeg

¼ cup brown sugar

Steps

1. Preheat the oven to 375°F.

2. Spray the baking dish with vegetable oil cooking spray.

3. Wash the apples. Using a knife on a cutting board, cut the apples in quarters and remove the core and all the seeds. Slice each quarter into 4 pieces.

4. In a large bowl, mix the lemon juice, flour, and cinnamon.

5. Toss in the apples and mix for 1 to 2 minutes.

6. Fill the baking pan with the apples.

7. Place the margarine in the microwave dish, cover, and cook at high for 30 to 60 seconds, until melted and bubbly.

8. Let cool for 1 minute before removing the cover. Pour the margarine into a medium bowl.

9. Add the flour, oats, cinnamon, nutmeg, and sugar to the margarine and mix. This will be the topping.

10. Sprinkle the topping over the apples.

11. Put the baking pan in the middle of the oven and bake for 45 minutes at 375° or until tender.

Time
20 minutes to prepare
plus
45 minutes to bake

Tools
8-inch square baking dish or pan

knife

cutting board

microwave dish with cover

large bowl

medium bowl

Makes
8 servings

CHAPTER 17

REAL FAT OR FAKE FAT?

Did you know that there is a frozen dessert that tastes like ice cream but contains no fat? Well, there is! Simple Pleasures® is a frozen dessert made with Simplesse, the first fat substitute approved by the Food and Drug Administration (the government agency that makes sure food is safe to eat). Legally, Simple Pleasures® can't be called ice cream because the FDA's standards require that ice cream contain at least 10 percent butterfat, so it is called a frozen dairy dessert.

Simplesse is made from egg white and milk protein blended and heated in a process called *microparticulation*. The aim of the process is to create the feel of a creamy liquid with the texture of fat. Because it is made from protein, it does contain calories, although only a little more than 1 calorie per gram because of its high water content.

Simple Pleasures® has about the same number of calories as regular ice cream because it contains more sugar and protein, but it has about half the calories of premium ice creams. Premium ice creams are very high in fat.

Simplesse may start appearing in other foods besides ice cream, such as mayonnaise, salad dressings, yogurt,

dips, sour cream, butter, margarine, and cheese spreads. Simplesse can't be used in cooking because heat causes it to lose its creaminess.

In baking, it is often possible to substitute applesauce or prune butter for fat. The recipes in this chapter use these ingredients in place of oil, margarine, or shortening. Bake them and see what you think!

TASTEBUD TEST

Materials
Simple Pleasures® Frozen Dessert
regular ice cream in same flavor as Simple Pleasures®
ice cream scoop
2 small bowls
a helper

Procedure

1. Ask a helper to place a scoop of Simple Pleasures in one bowl and a scoop of ice cream in the other bowl. Tell the helper not to let you know which is which.

2. Look at and taste each sample. Can you tell which is the real ice cream?

What Happened?
You were probably able to correctly identify which ice cream was regular ice cream and which was fat free. Fatty foods feel a certain way in your mouth, and fat-free versions often don't taste the same.

EXPERIMENT

Purpose
To compare the taste and texture of real fat versus fake fat.

•••• Fudge Brownies ••••

Time
15 minutes to prepare
plus
35 to 40 minutes to bake

Tools
8-inch square baking pan

wooden spoon

medium bowl

large bowl

whisk

rubber spatula

Makes
12 servings

This recipe substitutes applesauce for oil or margarine, which are fats.

Ingredients

vegetable oil cooking spray

½ cup unsweetened cocoa powder

¾ cup all-purpose flour

1 teaspoon baking powder

½ teaspoon salt

2 tablespoons margarine

1½ cups sugar

2 egg whites

½ cup applesauce

1 teaspoon vanilla extract

Steps

1. Preheat oven to 350°F.
2. Spray the baking pan with vegetable oil cooking spray.
3. In a medium bowl, mix cocoa powder, flour, baking powder, and salt.
4. With a wooden spoon, mix the margarine and sugar in a large bowl by pressing them against the side of the bowl.
5. Whisk the egg whites, applesauce, and vanilla extract into the margarine mixture.
6. Slowly mix the flour mixture into the egg mixture until combined.
7. Pour the batter into the baking pan. Spread evenly with the rubber spatula.
8. Bake for 35 to 40 minutes at 350°F or until firm.
9. Remove the pan from the oven and cool.
10. Cut the brownies into squares.

Slim-and-Trim Chocolate Chip Cookies

Prune butter does not contain any fat—only prunes and sugar. In this recipe, we've substituted prune butter for real butter.

Ingredients

1 cup prune butter

¾ cup light brown sugar

¾ cup sugar

2 eggs

2 teaspoons vanilla extract

2 cups all-purpose flour

1 teaspoon baking powder

1 teaspoon baking soda

1 teaspooon salt

¾ cup chocolate chips

Steps

1. Preheat oven to 350°F.

2. In a large bowl, combine the prune butter, brown sugar, sugar, eggs, and vanilla extract and whisk until well blended.

3. Sift together flour, baking powder, baking soda, and salt in a medium bowl.

4. Add the flour mixture to the large bowl with the prune butter. Stir until moistened.

5. Add chocolate chips and finish stirring.

6. Refrigerate the dough for 1 hour.

7. Shape pieces of dough into small balls and flatten them on the cookie sheet with the bottom of a glass.

8. Bake at 350°F for 8 to 10 minutes or until slightly golden brown.

9. Using oven mitts, remove the cookie sheet from the oven and let the cookies cool for about 5 minutes.

10. Remove the cookies with a spatula.

Time
15 minutes to prepare
plus
8 to 10 minutes to bake

Tools
large bowl

sifter

medium bowl

cookie sheets

drinking glass

spatula

Makes
4 dozen

CHAPTER 18

ALL THAT SUGAR!

There are many different forms of sugar at the supermarket: white sugar, brown sugar, powdered or confectioners' sugar, corn syrup, molasses, and fructose. There are really only two basic kinds of sugar: natural sugars and refined sugars. Natural sugars occur naturally in foods. Glucose, fructose, and honey are examples of natural sugars. Glucose is a part of the blood in your body, providing energy to all your body's cells. Fructose is called *fruit sugar* because it is found in ripe fruits. Honey is made by bees.

The most well-known refined sugar is table sugar, which contains both glucose and fructose. Other names for table sugar include white sugar, granulated sugar, and sucrose (its chemical name). If you look closely at table sugar, you will notice that it's a **crystal,** which is a **molecule** of chemicals arranged in an even shape. It is crystallized from the juice of the sugarcane plant or the sugar beet. Powdered, or confectioners', sugar is table sugar that has been ground to make it fine and powdery. Molasses is the thick brown syrup left over after making sugar from sugar cane. Brown sugar is a mixture of white sugar and molasses.

Corn syrup is thick and sweet. It is made from cornstarch and is often used in baked goods. High-fructose corn syrup is corn syrup that has been chemically changed to be sweeter than ordinary corn syrup by increasing the amount of fructose in it.

This chapter includes four cookie recipes, each using a different type of sugar.

MAKING SUGAR CRYSTALS

Materials

1 cup water
small saucepan
2 cups sugar
12-inch piece of string
straw
paper clip
glass jar
magnifying lens

Purpose

To demonstrate the growth of sugar crystals.

Procedure

1. Put one cup of water in the saucepan. Place on high heat and bring to a boil.

2. Add sugar and stir until no more sugar will dissolve.

3. Remove the saucepan from the burner and turn the heat off. Let cool for 10 minutes.

4. Tie one end of the string to the straw. Tie the paper clip to the other end of the string so that the clip just dangles above the bottom of the jar when the straw is placed over the top of the jar.

5. Drop the end of the string with the paper clip into the jar and lay the straw across the top of the jar.

6. Pour the sugar water into the jar. Put the jar in a place where it won't be disturbed for 7 days.

7. Look in the jar with your magnifying lens. What do you find?

What Happened?

When sugar dissolves, it doesn't really disappear. The sugar just breaks up into smaller and smaller pieces, until you can't see it. When you mix something with a liquid, it is called a *solution*. Hot water can hold more sugar than cold water. As your sugar/water solution cooled, sugar came out of the solution and formed crystals on the string.

This cookie mix is easy to make and is used to make the cookie recipes that follow. When you have a batch of this mix in the refrigerator, it's a snap to bake up your favorite cookies whenever you like.

Time
15 minutes

Tools
cutting board

large bowl

pastry blender
or
2 table knives

storage container
with lid

Makes
14 cups (about 5 batches
of cookies)

Ingredients

2 cups margarine

4½ cups all-purpose flour

4½ cups all-purpose flour

2 cups powdered milk

⅓ cup baking powder

¼ cup sugar

1 tablespoon salt

Steps

1. Using a table knife on a cutting board, cut the margarine into small pieces. Put margarine in a large bowl.

2. Add 4½ cups flour to the bowl with the margarine.

3. Holding a table knife in each hand, draw the knives across each other to cut through the margarine and dry ingredients. If using a pastry blender, cut through the margarine and dry ingredients. Keep cutting until the flour and fat mixture is in pieces about the size of peas.

4. Add 4½ cups flour, powdered milk, baking powder, sugar, and salt to the flour and fat mixture.

5. Pour the mix into a container with a tight lid and put it into the refrigerator. The mix can be stored in the refrigerator for up to 5 weeks.

Peanut Butter Cookie Treats

This recipe uses white sugar.

Time
15 minutes to prepare
plus
10 minutes to bake

Tools
plastic wrap

medium bowl

2 cookie sheets

drinking glass

fork

Makes
2 dozen cookies

Ingredients

1 tablespoon shortening

⅓ cup peanut butter

⅔ cup sugar

1 egg

1 teaspoon vanilla extract

1 tablespoon water

1½ cups Power Cookie Mix

3 tablespoons sugar

Steps

1. Preheat the oven to 375°F.

2. Pick up the shortening with a piece of plastic wrap or wax paper and rub it on the cookie sheets.

3. Mix the peanut butter and sugar together in a medium bowl.

4. Add the egg, vanilla extract, and water to the peanut butter mixture. Stir well.

5. Add the Power Cookie Mix to the peanut butter mixture and stir well.

6. Roll the dough into 1-inch balls.

7. Roll the balls in sugar.

8. Flatten the balls with the bottom of a drinking glass.

9. Place the pieces of cookie dough on a cookie sheet and make an *X* with the tines of a fork on the top of each piece of dough.

10. Bake at 375°F for about 8 to 10 minutes or until golden brown.

11. Using oven mitts, remove the cookie sheet from the oven and let the cookies cool for about 5 minutes.

12. Remove the cookies with a spatula.

M&M® Cookies

This recipe uses brown sugar.

Ingredients

1 tablespoon shortening

3 cups Power Cookie Mix

¾ cup dark brown sugar

1 egg

⅓ cup water

½ teaspoon vanilla extract

1½ cups M&M® brand chocolate candies

Steps

1. Preheat the oven to 375°F.

2. Pick up the shortening with a piece of plastic wrap or wax paper and rub it on the cookie sheet.

3. Place the Power Cookie Mix in a medium bowl. Set aside.

4. Mix dark brown sugar, egg, water, and vanilla extract together in a small bowl.

5. Add the sugar-egg mixture to the Power Cookie Mix and stir just until well blended.

6. Fold M&Ms® into Power Cookie Mix.

7. Drop the cookie batter by teaspoonfuls onto cookie sheet.

8. Bake at 375° for about 8 to 10 minutes or until golden brown. After 5 minutes, switch cookie pan positions in oven for even baking.

9. Using oven mitts, remove the cookie sheet from the oven and let the cookies cool for about 5 minutes.

10. Remove the cookies with a spatula.

Variations

Chocolate Chip Cookies   Instead of M&Ms®, use 1½ cups of chocolate chips.

Peanut Butter Chip Cookies   Instead of M&Ms®, use 1½ cups of peanut butter chips.

Apple Raisin Cookies   Instead of M&Ms®, use 1 cup diced fresh apple and ½ cup raisins.

Time
15 minutes to prepare
plus
10 minutes to bake

Tools
plastic wrap

medium bowl

small bowl

2 cookie sheets

teaspoon

Makes
3 dozen cookies

Major Molasses Cookie Bites

Time
15 minutes to prepare
plus
10 minutes to bake

Tools
plastic wrap
medium bowl
small bowl
whip
teaspoon
cookie sheets

Makes
4 dozen cookies

• • • • •
Cloves *are the unopened flower buds of a tropical evergreen tree.*
• • • • •

This recipe uses mostly molasses for sweetening.

Ingredients

1 tablespoon shortening
4 cups Power Cookie Mix
¼ cup sugar
½ cup brown sugar
1 teaspoon cinnamon

1 teaspoon ginger
½ teaspoon cloves
1 egg
1 cup molasses

Steps

1. Preheat the oven to 375°F.

2. Pick up the shortening with a piece of plastic wrap or wax paper and rub it on cookie sheets.

3. Put the Power Cookie Mix, sugar, brown sugar, cinnamon, ginger, and cloves in a medium bowl. Mix until combined.

4. Whisk together the egg and molasses in a small bowl until well blended.

5. Put the egg mixture into the bowl with the mix. Stir just until well blended.

6. Drop cookie batter by teaspoonfuls onto cookie sheet.

7. Bake at 375°F for about 8 to 10 minutes or until golden brown.

8. Using oven mitts, remove the cookie sheet from the oven and let the cookies cool for about 5 minutes.

9. Remove the cookies with a spatula.

Delicious Double-Chocolate Honey Brownies

This recipe uses honey as the sweetener.

Ingredients

1 tablespoon shortening
1 cup Power Cookie Mix
⅔ cup honey
½ cup unsweetened cocoa
¼ cup margarine

1 egg
¼ cup water
1 teaspoon vanilla extract
1 cup mini chocolate chips
or
1 cup M&M® brand chocolate candies

Time
15 minutes to prepare
plus
20 minutes to bake

Tools
plastic wrap

9-inch square pan

medium bowl

small microwave dish
with lid

Makes
25 brownies

Steps

1. Preheat the oven to 350°F.

2. Pick up the shortening with a piece of plastic wrap or wax paper and rub it on bottom and sides of pan.

3. Put the Power Cookie Mix, honey, and cocoa in a medium bowl. Mix well.

4. Place margarine in the microwave dish and cover.

5. Cook the margarine on the high setting for 30 to 60 seconds, until melted and bubbly.

6. Let cool for 1 minute before removing cover.

7. Add the margarine, egg, water, and vanilla extract to the bowl with the mix. Mix thoroughly.

8. Fold chocolate chips or M&Ms® into the batter.

9. Pour the batter into the pan.

10. Bake at 350°F about 20 minutes or until lightly browned.

11. Cool before cutting into squares.

CHAPTER 19

WHICH CEREAL HAS MORE FIBER?

Fiber is not a single substance but a variety of substances. What is unique about fiber is that it can't be digested in your body. In other words, most fiber passes through your stomach and intestines unchanged and is excreted. This feature of fiber is important because it helps our bodies to process and excrete other solid waste.

Fiber is found only in plant foods, where it supports the plant's stems, leaves, and seeds. Fiber is in fruits, dried beans and peas, grains, and vegetables. Fiber is *not* found in animal foods such as meat, poultry, fish, dairy products, and eggs.

There are two major types of fiber: soluble and insoluble. Soluble fiber dissolves in water, where it forms a gel much like gelatin. Pectin, a soluble fiber, is particularly helpful in making jam, as you will see in the following experiment. Insoluble fiber does not dissolve in water.

Many of the cereals at the supermarket have the words "high fiber" written on them in large letters. Some breakfast cereals can be an excellent source of fiber. To tell which cereal has the most fiber, look for the "Nutrition Facts" section on the box. Here you will find the number of grams of fiber in one serving of the cereal. Nutrition experts recommend that you eat 25 grams of fiber daily. Many cereals provide 3 grams or more per serving.

The recipes in this section focus on high-fiber foods, such as wheat bran (the outer layer of the wheat kernel), dried beans, and lentils.

MAKING JAM WITH PECTIN

Materials

4 cups blackberries, raspberries, or strawberries (remove hulls of strawberries)

4 cups sugar

¼ teaspoon finely shredded lemon peel

half of a 6-ounce package (1 foil pouch) liquid fruit pectin

2 tablespoons lemon juice

medium bowl

small bowl

4 half-pint freezer containers

spoon

Purpose

To show the effect of pectin on crushed fruit.

Procedure

1. Crush berries.

2. Measure 2 cups crushed blackberries or raspberries or 1¾ cups strawberries and place in large bowl.

3. Add sugar and lemon peel to crushed fruit. Let stand 10 minutes.

4. Combine pectin and lemon juice in small bowl.

5. Add pectin–lemon juice mixture to crushed fruit. Stir for 3 minutes.

6. Spoon crushed fruit right away into freezer containers up to ½ inch from the top. Seal.

7. Let freezer containers stand at room temperature about 2 hours or until jam is set.

8. Store up to 3 weeks in the refrigerator or 1 year in the freezer.

What Happened?

Jam gets its semisolid consistency from pectin, a form of fiber. The long, stringlike pectin molecules thicken the fruit mixture by bonding to each other. This bonding makes a kind of net that traps the liquid from the fruit and gives jam its consistency. Some fruits, such as grapes, are rich enough in pectin to make their own jam. Other fruits need to have pectin added.

Bran muffins are a great source of fiber at breakfast or snack time.

Ingredients

vegetable oil cooking spray

1	cup water	1	cup raisins
3	cups unprocessed bran	2½	teaspoons baking soda
2	eggs	½	teaspoon salt
2	cups buttermilk	⅓	cup sugar
	or	1	cup all-purpose flour
2	cups nonfat plain yogurt	1½	cups whole wheat flour
½	cup vegetable oil		

Time
25 minutes to prepare
plus
20 minutes to bake

Tools
2 muffin pans

small saucepan

large bowl

2 medium bowls

wooden spoon

oven mitts

Makes
24 muffins

Steps

1. Preheat the oven to 425°F.

2. Spray muffin pans with vegetable oil cooking spray, or use nonstick muffin pans.

3. Put water in small saucepan and put on high heat. Bring to a boil.

4. Mix bran and boiling water together in a large bowl. Stir to moisten evenly and set aside to cool.

5. In a medium bowl, mix the eggs, buttermilk or yogurt, oil, and raisins. Stir into the bran mixture.

6. In another medium bowl, stir together the baking soda, salt, sugar, all-purpose flour, and whole wheat flour. Stir into the bran mixture.

7. Using a large spoon, fill each muffin cup two-thirds full with batter.

8. Bake at 425°F for 20 minutes.

9. Using oven mitts, remove the pan from the oven and let cool for 10 minutes on a cooling rack.

10. Remove muffins from pan.

•••••
Bran *is the outer layer of a grain kernel, such as wheat. Wheat bran is an excellent source of fiber.*
•••••

Baked Beans with Apples

Time
20 to 25 minutes
to prepare
plus
30 minutes to cook

Tools
knife

cutting board

large frying pan

colander

2-quart casserole

Makes
8 servings

Beans, like those used to make baked beans, are one of the best sources of fiber. This recipe is a little sweeter than most baked bean recipes.

Ingredients

1 medium onion
2 apples
vegetable oil cooking spray
1 16-oz. can black beans
1 16-oz. can pinto beans

1 16-oz. can navy beans
⅓ cup ketchup
3 tablespoons brown sugar
2 tablespoons molasses
1 tablespoon spicy brown mustard

Steps

1. Preheat the oven to 350°F.
2. Remove the outer skin from the onion. Using a knife on a cutting board, cut the onion in half and chop.
3. Wash and dry the apples.
4. Cut apples in half on a cutting board and remove the seeds. Chop the apples.
5. Spray a large frying pan with cooking spray.
6. Heat frying pan over medium heat for one minute.
7. Cook onions and apples in frying pan until onions and apples are soft, about 5 minutes.
8. Open the cans of black beans, pinto beans, and navy beans.
9. Empty the cans of beans into a colander to drain.
10. In a 2-quart casserole, stir together apple and onion mixture, beans, ketchup, brown sugar, molasses, and mustard.
11. Put casserole in 350°F oven and bake 30 minutes, or until bubbly.

Lentil Burritos

*If you like to roll up your dinner in a tortilla,
try this recipe.*

Ingredients

1 medium onion
1 cup lentils
2 cups water
½ teaspoon ground cumin
1 dash hot pepper sauce
1 tomato

1 green or sweet red pepper
1 cup mild taco sauce
8 small flour tortillas
4 oz. shredded low-fat
mozzarella cheese

Time
30 minutes

Tools
knife

cutting board

colander

medium saucepan

microwave plate

paper towel

Makes
8 burritos

Steps

1. Remove the outer skin from the onion. Using a knife on a cutting board, cut the onion in half and chop.
2. Wash the lentils in a colander.
3. Place the lentils and onion in a medium saucepan. Add water, cumin, and hot pepper sauce.
4. Put saucepan on stove and set heat to high. Bring to a boil.
5. Reduce heat to low-medium and simmer 15 to 20 minutes, just until the lentils are tender.
6. While the lentils are cooking, wash the tomato and pepper.
7. Using a knife on a cutting board, cut the tomato and pepper in half.
8. Remove the seeds from the pepper.
9. Chop the tomato and pepper.
10. When the lentils are tender, add the tomatoes, peppers, and taco sauce and heat through.
11. Put a stack of 8 tortillas on a microwave plate and cover with a moist paper towel. Heat on high in the microwave for 40 seconds or until warm.
12. To make the burritos, spoon ½ cup of lentils down the middle of each tortilla.
13. Sprinkle cheese on top of lentil mixture and roll up each burrito.

*When rinsing lentils,
be sure to remove
anything that's not a
lentil, such as pebbles,
that might have
gotten mixed in.*

CHAPTER 20

WHITE RICE OR BROWN RICE?

Rice is one of many kinds of grain. Grains are the seeds of cultivated grasses, such as rice, wheat, or oats. All grains have a similar structure that includes layers of bran, an endosperm, and a germ. The *endosperm* is the large central area of the grain. It contains mostly starch. At one end of the endosperm is the germ.

The *germ* is a good source of oil and vitamin E. The *bran*, which is full of fiber, covers both the endosperm and the germ.

A seed contains everything needed to reproduce the plant: the germ is the embryo from which a new plant will grow, the endosperm contains the nutrients for growth, and the bran protects it.

— bran

— endosperm

— germ

Rice, like most grains, undergoes processing or milling after harvesting. The most common form of rice is white rice. To make white rice, the outer hull of the grain is removed, and the layers of bran are milled, or ground away, until the grain is white. If just the outer hull of the grain is removed (it's inedible anyway!) but the bran is left on, the rice is called brown

rice. Brown rice gets its name from its tan-brown color. While white rice is rather bland in flavor, brown rice has a nutlike flavor and a chewy texture. Brown rice also takes longer to cook than white rice because the bran layers act as a barrier to cooking.

Rice is an excellent source of carbohydrates and contains only a trace of fat and no cholesterol. Brown rice, because it is a whole grain, contains more nutrients (such as fiber and vitamin E) than white rice.

Other rices you may see at the store are basmati rice and wild rice. Basmati rice is a flavorful variety of rice with a unique nutty flavor that goes well with Indian food. Wild rice is not a true rice. It is a grass that grows wild in the Great Lakes region of the United States. Wild rice is dark brown in color and has a nutty flavor.

Rice is cooked by stirring it into boiling water, then reducing the heat to a simmer, covering, and cooking until the liquid is absorbed. Regular white rice takes about 20 minutes to cook. You can buy precooked or instant white rice that cooks up in less time. Although this type of rice cooks quickly, the grains will become mushy if overcooked.

Another type of white rice is called *parboiled* or *converted* rice. Parboiled rice has been partially cooked under steam pressure, then dried and milled to remove the outer hull and bran. The parboiling process results in a grain that is more nutritious than regular white rice but takes a little longer to cook (about 25 minutes).

COOKING WHITE RICE AND BROWN RICE

Purpose

To compare the cooking times of white and brown rice.

Materials

2 saucepans with lids
½ cup white rice (parboiled)
½ cup brown rice
plate

Procedure

1. Put 1 cup of water and white rice in one saucepan.

2. Put 1 cup of water and brown rice in the other saucepan.

3. Bring both saucepans to a boil over high heat. Lower heat and simmer, covered, for 25 minutes.

4. Put a small amount of rice on a plate. Does either taste tender and ready to eat? Does either need more cooking?

What Happened?

After 25 minutes of cooking, the white rice will be tender but the brown rice will be quite crunchy. Brown rice takes longer to cook because the bran on the outside of each kernel acts as a barrier to heat and cooking.

Fruited Rice

This recipe is a nice change from plain rice.

Time
30 to 60 minutes
(depending on type of rice)

Ingredients

1 cup rice, brown or white

3 apples

1 tablespoon vegetable oil

½ cup raisins

1 tablespoon sesame seeds (optional)

Tools
medium saucepan
with lid

knife

cutting board

small frying pan

spatula

spoon

Makes
4 servings

Steps

1. Cook the rice according to the package instructions.

2. While the rice is cooking, wash the apples. Using a knife on a cutting board, cut the apples in half. Remove the core and all the seeds.

3. Slice the apples.

4. Put the oil in a small frying pan put on medium heat. When the oil is hot, add the apples.

5. Cook for 5 minutes, then turn apples with a spatula. Cook apples for 5 more minutes.

6. Stir in raisins and cooked rice. Cook, stirring constantly, until the rice is heated through.

7. Spoon the rice out onto plates; top with sesame seeds if you like.

•••••••••••••• Creamy Chicken on Rice ••••••••••••

Time
30 to 60 minutes
(depending on type of
rice)

Tools
medium saucepan
with lid

knife

cutting board

small saucepan

Makes
4 servings

This is a great way to use up leftover chicken.

Ingredients

1 cup rice, brown or white

leftover cooked chicken, 1 cup

1 can cream of mushroom
soup (10½ ounces)

Steps

1. Cook rice according to package instructions in a
   medium saucepan.

2. Using a knife on a cutting board, cut the chicken into
   bite-sized pieces.

3. Put chicken and soup in a small saucepan. Mix
   together and heat on medium. Simmer gently for 10
   minutes until heated through.

4. Spoon the rice onto plates and serve the chicken-soup
   mixture over the rice.

NUTRITION IN A NUTSHELL

Nutrition is about you and food. It is the food you eat and how the body uses it. You need food to get energy for play, to breathe, and to keep your heart beating. The energy in food is called **calories.** Food also provides a variety of substances called **nutrients** that are needed to help you grow, to repair your body, and to keep you healthy.

A booklet from the U.S. Department of Agriculture and the U.S. Department for Health and Human Services called *Dietary Guidelines for Americans* provides the following answers to the question "What should we be eating to stay healthy?"

1. *Eat a variety of foods.* You need more than 40 different nutrients for good health.

2. *Maintain a healthy weight.* If you are too fat or too thin, your chances of developing health problems are increased. To lose weight, you need to eat fewer calories (calories tell us how much energy is packed in each food).

3. *Choose a diet low in **fat** and **cholesterol**.* Fat is a nutrient that supplies more energy than any other nutrient. People who eat diets high in fat are more likely to have heart disease and certain types of cancer than people who don't. Some fats you eat you can actually see—such as margarine, vegetable oil, and butter. But many other fats are not so obvious—such as the fat in hamburgers, in whole milk and many cheeses, in cookies, cakes, fried foods, mayonnaise, salad dressings, and more foods. Cholesterol is a fat-like nutrient made in the body and found in every cell. Eggs and liver contain the highest amounts of cholesterol found in foods.

4. *Eat plenty of vegetables, fruits, and grain products, such as breads, cereals, pasta, and rice.* These foods are generally low in fats. By choosing them often, you are likely to decrease fats and increase **carbohydrates** in your diet. Carbohydrates are a group of nutrients that include sugar, starch, and **fiber.** Fiber is found only in plant foods such as fruits, vegetables, and grains. Eating fiber has many desirable effects.

5. *Don't use a lot of sugar.* Sugars and foods that contain them in large amounts supply calories but few nutrients. Therefore, people don't need much sugar and it can add unnecessary weight.

6. *Don't use a lot of salt and sodium.* Table salt contains sodium and chlorine—two minerals needed in your diet. However, most Americans eat more salt and sodium than they need. Sodium is also added to a lot of foods during processing. Always check the labels carefully before you buy.

THE FOOD GUIDE PYRAMID

Another way to look at what we need to eat each day is pictured in the accompanying illustration, the Food Guide Pyramid. The Food Guide Pyramid emphasizes foods from the five food groups shown in the three lower sections. Each of these food groups provides some, but not all, of the nutrients you need. Foods in one group can't replace those in another. No one food group is more important than another—for good health, you need them all. But you need more of some groups, such as bread, than others, such as fats. Also, vary your choices of foods within each group because specific foods differ in the kinds and amounts of nutrients they provide.

The Food Guide Pyramid
A Guide to Daily Food Choices

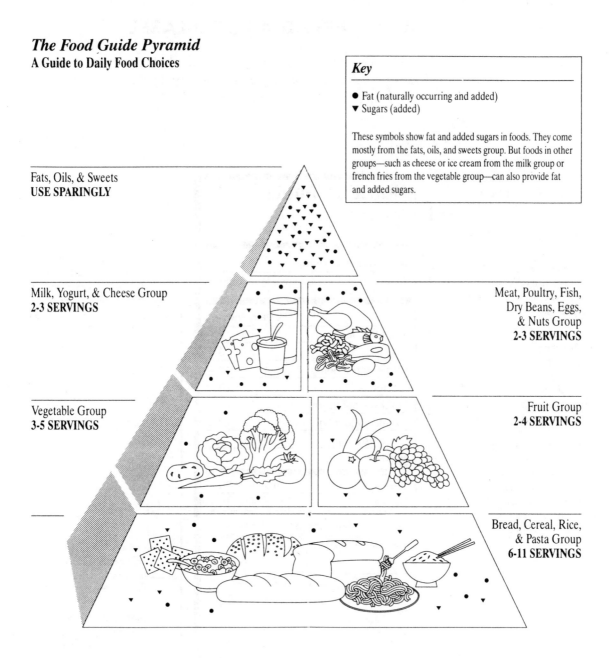

Key

● Fat (naturally occurring and added)
▼ Sugars (added)

These symbols show fat and added sugars in foods. They come mostly from the fats, oils, and sweets group. But foods in other groups—such as cheese or ice cream from the milk group or french fries from the vegetable group—can also provide fat and added sugars.

Fats, Oils, & Sweets
USE SPARINGLY

Milk, Yogurt, & Cheese Group
2-3 SERVINGS

Meat, Poultry, Fish, Dry Beans, Eggs, & Nuts Group
2-3 SERVINGS

Vegetable Group
3-5 SERVINGS

Fruit Group
2-4 SERVINGS

Bread, Cereal, Rice, & Pasta Group
6-11 SERVINGS

HOW TO READ A FOOD LABEL

Ever notice that little section of the food label called Nutrition Facts on the foods you buy at the supermarket? Let's check it out—from top to bottom—on a frozen dinner.

The serving size is 12 ounces—that's ¾ pound. This package has 1 serving in it, so you'd have to eat all the food in the package to get the amounts of the nutrients listed.

There are 340 calories in the serving, and 45 of those calories come from fat. That doesn't seem bad at all.

The nutrients listed are those most important to the health of the average American. You should try to eat 100% of your carbohydrate, fiber, vitamin, and mineral values in one day, over several meals. You should keep down the percentage of fat, saturated fat, cholesterol, and sodium. This food is not too high in fat and cholesterol and is a good source of fiber, protein, and vitamin C.

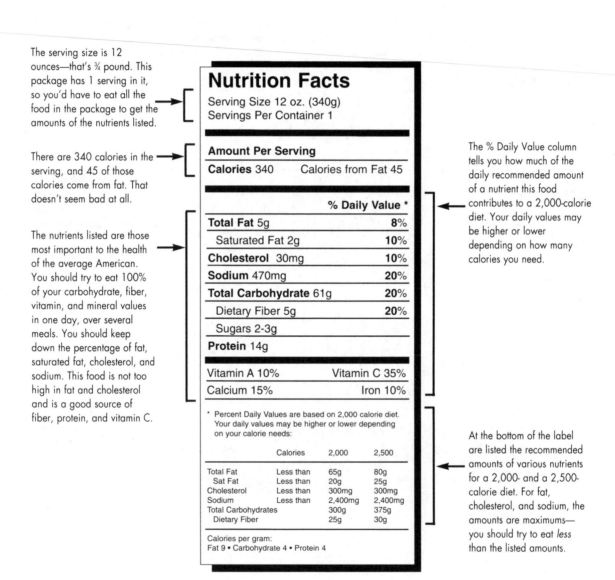

Nutrition Facts

Serving Size 12 oz. (340g)
Servings Per Container 1

Amount Per Serving

Calories 340   Calories from Fat 45

	% Daily Value *
Total Fat 5g	**8%**
Saturated Fat 2g	**10%**
Cholesterol 30mg	**10%**
Sodium 470mg	**20%**
Total Carbohydrate 61g	**20%**
Dietary Fiber 5g	**20%**
Sugars 2-3g	
Protein 14g	

Vitamin A 10%	Vitamin C 35%
Calcium 15%	Iron 10%

* Percent Daily Values are based on 2,000 calorie diet. Your daily values may be higher or lower depending on your calorie needs:

		Calories	2,000	2,500
Total Fat	Less than		65g	80g
Sat Fat	Less than		20g	25g
Cholesterol	Less than		300mg	300mg
Sodium	Less than		2,400mg	2,400mg
Total Carbohydrates			300g	375g
Dietary Fiber			25g	30g

Calories per gram:
Fat 9 • Carbohydrate 4 • Protein 4

The % Daily Value column tells you how much of the daily recommended amount of a nutrient this food contributes to a 2,000-calorie diet. Your daily values may be higher or lower depending on how many calories you need.

At the bottom of the label are listed the recommended amounts of various nutrients for a 2,000- and a 2,500- calorie diet. For fat, cholesterol, and sodium, the amounts are maximums— you should try to eat *less* than the listed amounts.

NUTRIENT CONTENT OF RECIPES

This table shows the amount of calories, fat, cholesterol, fiber, and sodium contained in one serving of each recipe in this book. You can compare these numbers to how much you need daily.

Recipe	Serving Size	Calories	Fat (grams)	Cholesterol (milligrams)	Fiber (grams)	Sodium (milligrams)
Chapter 1						
The Best Popcorn	2 cups	98	5	0	1	0
Rosy Popcorn	2 cups	131	9	0	1	106
Raisin Popcorn Squares	1 square	110	4	0	0.5	49
Trail Mix Popcorn	1 cup	111	4	0	1.6	75
Cheddar-Cheese-and-Chive Popcorn	2 cups	134	10	7	0.7	127
Popcorn Santa Fe	1 square	63	4	6	0.2	180
Holiday Popcorn Balls	1 ball	230	9	0	1	111
Chapter 2						
French Onion Soup	1 cup	252	12	12	2	912
Chapter 3						
Nutmeg-and-Brown-Sugar Toast	2 slices	290	10	0	3	301
Old-Fashioned Cinnamon Toast	2 slices	290	10	0	3	301
Peanut-Butter-and-Jelly French Toast Cut-Outs	1 sandwich	323	11	54	4	332

Recipe	Serving Size	Calories	Fat (grams)	Cholesterol (milligrams)	Fiber (grams)	Sodium (milligrams)
Linzer Tart French Toast	1 sandwich	248	3	55	4	271
Individual Fruit-and-Cheesecake Toast Tarts	1	395	8	22	3	645
Strawberry Butter	1 tbsp.	74	7	0	1	90
Creamy Herb-and-Chive Spread	1 tbsp.	16	2	5	0	14

Chapter 4

Recipe	Serving Size	Calories	Fat (grams)	Cholesterol (milligrams)	Fiber (grams)	Sodium (milligrams)
Basic Baked Potatoes	1 potato	220	0	0	5	16
Broccoli-and-Cheddar Stuffed Potatoes	1 potato	398	13	40	5	277
Smashed Potatoes	½ cup	115	6	0	1	77
Fabulous Baked Fries	¾ cup	157	13	0	3	77
Potato Skins with Cheddar and Salsa	1 skin	79	2	6	1	65

Chapter 5

Recipe	Serving Size	Calories	Fat (grams)	Cholesterol (milligrams)	Fiber (grams)	Sodium (milligrams)
Oodles of Noodles and Cheese	1 svg.	642	27	68	0	542
Simple Low-Fat Cheese Sauce	½ cup	160	6	24	0	472

Chapter 6

Recipe	Serving Size	Calories	Fat (grams)	Cholesterol (milligrams)	Fiber (grams)	Sodium (milligrams)
Summer Fruit Salad	1 svg.	117	3	0	3	25
Winter Fruit Salad	1 svg.	63	0	0	2	1
Fruit Kabobs	1 kabob	74	0.4	0	2	3

Recipe	Serving Size	Calories	Fat (grams)	Cholesterol (milligrams)	Fiber (grams)	Sodium (milligrams)
Chapter 7						
White Bread	1 slice	58	0	0	0.5	134
Basic Pizza Dough	⅛ recipe	163	4	0	1	267
Possibilities Pizza	⅛ recipe	352	15	24	2	742
Stromboli Pizzoli	⅛ recipe	288	14	16	1	588
Monkey Bread	1 svg.	477	15	0	3	755
Chapter 8						
Baking Powder Biscuits	1 biscuit	117	4	0.5	0.5	221
Blueberry Bear Pancakes	1 pancake	101	3	30	0.5	175
Basic Muffins	1 muffin	167	5	18	1	264
Chapter 9						
Meringue Shells	1 shell	44	0	0	0	14
Angel Food Cake	½ cake	142	0	0	0	138
Fluffy Omelet	1 svg.	155	10	426	0	134
Chapter 10						
Italian Dressing	1 tbsp.	65	7	0	0	0
Raspberry Dressing	1 tbsp.	17	2	0	0	36
Thousand Island Dressing	1 tbsp.	39	3	3	0	77
Russian Dressing	1 tbsp.	30	3	3	0	34
Honey-Yogurt Dressing	1 tbsp.	14	0	1	0	8
Tuny Salad	1 svg.	227	9	46	0	507
Waldorf Salad	1 svg.	123	5	5	3	37
Three-Bean Salad	1 svg.	88	4	0	3	24

Recipe	Serving Size	Calories	Fat (grams)	Cholesterol (milligrams)	Fiber (grams)	Sodium (milligrams)
Chapter 11						
Tomato Sauce	½ cup	19	0	0	1	7
Primavera Sauce	½ cup	78	0	1.7	3	164
Blender Pesto Sauce	1 ounce	155	15	14	0	244
Chapter 12						
Fruited Parfaits	1 cup	116	1	4	1	110
The All-American Cheeseburger	1 cheese-burger	350	19	63	1	338
Chapter 13						
Homemade Whipped Cream	¼ cup	103	11	42	0	11
Homemade Buttercream Frosting	¼ cup	320	11	31	0	253
Basic Cupcakes	1	172	7	18	0	143
Chapter 14						
Nilla Vanilla Pudding	½ cup	101	4	1	0	95
The Richest Chocolate Pudding	½ cup	125	6	1	0	95
Rich Caramel Pudding	½ cup	145	6	4	0	111
Fruit 'n Pudding Sundae	1 sundae	221	11	28	1	104
Chapter 15						
Fruisicles	1 pop	43	0	0	0	3
Yogurt Fruisicles	1 pop	75	0	1	0	57
Pudding Pops	1 pop	59	0	0	0	138

Recipe	Serving Size	Calories	Fat (grams)	Cholesterol (milligrams)	Fiber (grams)	Sodium (milligrams)
Chapter 16						
Watermelon Butterfly Salad	1 svg.	105	1	0	4	29
Baked Apples	1 apple	159	3	0	3	5
Apple Cobbler	⅛ recipe	230	6	0	6	53
Chapter 17						
Fudge Brownies	½ recipe	165	3	0	0	150
Slim-and-Trim Chocolate Chip Cookies	1 cookie	53	0	9	0	72
Chapter 18						
Peanut-Butter Cookie Treats	1 cookie	77	3	9	0	75
M&M® Cookies	1 cookie	86	4	6	0	77
Major Molasses Cookie Bites	1 cookie	66	2	5	0	77
Delicious Double-Chocolate Honey Brownies	1 square	95	5	9	0	70
Chapter 19						
Ready-Bake Bran Muffins	1 muffin	147	5	19	12	150
Baked Beans with Apples	¾ cup	203	1	0	2	597
Lentil Burritos	1 burrito	209	4	8	4	196

Recipe	Serving Size	Calories	Fat (grams)	Cholesterol (milligrams)	Fiber (grams)	Sodium (milligrams)
Chapter 20						
Fruited Rice	1 serving	314	4	0	4	5
Creamy Chicken on Rice	1 serving	438	13	90	0.5	475

C

WHAT'S SAFE TO EAT?

Even if you choose a very nutritious diet, there are still dangers lurking in your food. They seem to be reported on television and in the newspapers and magazines all the time. Are apples really sprayed with a dangerous chemical? Is eating an undercooked fast-food hamburger going to hospitalize you? Let's look at how to keep food safe.

FOOD POISONING

Foodborne illness, commonly called food poisoning, is caused by substances in food such as bacteria and molds, which make you sick to your stomach, but can be even more serious. Sometimes fever and infection occur. The symptoms may start within an hour of eating the suspected food or up to several days later.

Foodborne illness is most often caused by microorganisms. Microorganisms include bacteria and viruses. *Micro* means small, and both bacteria and viruses are so small that they cannot be seen by the naked eye. Bacteria are in the air, in the ground, and on you and me. Given the right temperature and enough time, bacteria will multiply in food (they double in number every 20 minutes). Bacteria cause foodborne illness when they multiply in food to the point that when the food is eaten, they make you very sick. Luckily, not all bacteria cause foodborne illness; only a small number do.

Bacteria grow readily under these three conditions.

1. **In a food that contains some protein,** such as meat, poultry, fish, eggs, dairy products, gravies and sauces, potato, beans, and rice.

2. **At a temperature between 45°F and 140°F.** Refrigeration is normally at or below 45°F, so bacteria grow slowly if at all. Bacterial growth slows down even more in the freezer, which is usually kept at or below 0°F. Room temperature is normally around 70°F—a great temperature for bacteria to grow.

3. For at least two hours in the temperature zone given in #2.

In some, but not all, cases, adequate cooking of the contaminated food (to 165°F) will prevent problems. However, cooking does not kill all forms of bacteria, and in many cases the contaminated food may not even be cooked further, as in the case of tuna salad.

Here are some ways to prevent foodborne illness in your home.

1. Keep hot foods hot and cold foods cold (below 45°F).

2. Wash your hands frequently, especially after handling raw meat, poultry, seafood, or eggs.

3. Don't touch yourself, while handling food, because bacteria on your skin can then be introduced into the food. Don't use your fingers to taste food—use a spoon.

4. Cover all cuts, burns, and boils with a waterproof bandage. Cuts, burns, and boils are the home to many bacteria that you don't want in your food.

5. Keep all equipment sparkling clean and wash after every use. For instance, if you use your cutting board for cutting chicken, wash it thoroughly with *hot* water and soap before cutting lettuce on it (wash your knife, too)!

6. Use a different spoon for stirring raw foods, such as meat that is being browned, and cooked foods.

7. Cook and reheat foods until they are very hot and well done.

8. Don't eat raw meat, fish, or eggs. They may contain harmful bacteria, viruses, or parasites. If a dough or batter contains raw eggs, don't eat it before it is cooked!

9. Thaw meats, poultry, and seafood in the refrigerator overnight. Don't leave them out to thaw.

These are good rules to follow. A final rule of thumb is: "When in doubt, throw it out." It's probably not worth getting sick about.

MOLDS

Ever notice a little bluish green fuzz growing on your tomatoes? You probably knew it was just mold, but wondered if you could just cut out the moldy spot or if you should throw out the entire tomato. Molds cause spoilage (most often of fruits and bread), musty odors, and yucky flavors in foods. Molds also grow on vegetables, meats, and cheese that have been exposed to the air. Although molds will be killed by most cooking, the toxins (poisons) they produce will not, so you need to avoid eating moldy food. In foods with a firm texture, such as potatoes and hard cheeses, you can just cut out the moldy area. When dealing with a soft food, such as bread or tomatoes, it is best to throw the food out if you find any mold on it.

To avoid a dangerous mold that grows on peanuts (and corn), it is best to buy national brands. Also, throw out any moldy peanuts, peanut butter, cornmeal, or other corn products.

PESTICIDES

Pesticides are chemicals used to control insects, diseases, weeds, fungi, mold, and other pests on plants, vegetables, fruits, and animals. Pesticides are normally applied to crops as a spray, fog, or dust.

The government allows a small amount of pesticides to be left on the food you buy, but to be safe, you should avoid eating them. Here's how.

- Buy organically grown fruits and vegetables (these are grown without the use of pesticides) when possible.
- Throw away the outer leaves of leafy vegetables such as lettuce.
- Wash fruits and vegetables carefully, using a brush.
- Peel carrots, waxed cucumbers, peaches, and pears, because these foods are more likely to have hazardous pesticide residues.
- Buy local produce, as it is probably treated with less pesticide than produce that has to travel a long distance.
- Trim fat and skin from meat, poultry, and fish. Pesticides in animal feed can concentrate in animal fat. Skim fat from pan drippings, broths, sauces, and soups.
- Eat a varied diet so that no one food dominates.

GLOSSARY

beat   To move the utensil back and forth to blend ingredients together.

blend   To mix two or more ingredients thoroughly until uniform.

boil   To be at the boiling point—212°F for water. When a liquid boils, that means it is turning into steam (the gaseous state of water).

calorie   A measure of the energy in food.

carbohydrate   A group of nutrients that include sugar, starch, and fiber.

cholesterol   A fatlike nutrient made in the body and found in every cell.

chop   To cut into irregularly sized pieces.

coagulate   To become firm.

cream   To mix margarine or butter and sugar (usually) by pressing them against the bowl with the back of a spoon until they look creamy.

crystal   A clear, solid substance that has smooth surfaces and is balanced in shape on all sides.

dice   To cut into cubes of the same size.

fat   A nutrient that supplies more energy than any other nutrient.

fiber   A variety of substances present in plant foods that can't be digested in the body.

fold   To mix ingredients using a gentle over-and-under motion with a utensil.

foodborne illness   A disease caused by substances in food, such as bacteria and molds, that make you sick.

gluten   An elastic substance in flour that gives bread its sturdy structure.

grate   To rub a food across a grater's tiny punched holes to produce small or fine pieces of food.

knead   To work dough into a smooth mass by pressing and folding.

mince   To chop very fine.

mix   To combine ingredients so that they are all evenly distributed.

molecule   Two or more atoms that form a substance with properties different from those of the atoms of which it is made.

nutrient   One of many substances in food that are needed for you to grow, to repair your body, and to keep you healthy.

nutrition   The science that explores the food you eat and how the body uses it.

pan-fry   To cook in a pan over moderate heat in a small amount of fat.

proof   To add yeast to warm water and sugar to make sure it's active.

protein   A nutrient that is needed for your body to grow and be healthy.

puree   To change a solid food into a thick liquid.

sauté   To cook quickly in a pan over medium-high heat in a small amount of fat.

shred   To rub a food across a surface with medium to large holes or slits to produce small pieces of food.

simmer   To cook in a liquid that is just below boiling.

slice   To cut into uniform slices.

sodium   A mineral present in salt, which is needed by your body.

steam   To cook with steam.

whip   To beat rapidly using a circular motion, usually with a wire whip, to incorporate air into the mixture (such as in making whipped cream).

whisk   To beat ingredients together with a wire whip until they are well blended.

yeast   A tiny, single-celled organism that makes bread dough rise.

INDEX

C

D

Vegetables
  in diet, 157
  dips and spreads for, 129
  and pesticides, 167
  for Primavera Sauce, 100
Vinegar, 86–89, 95
Vitamin C, 39, 55, 56

Waldorf Salad, 94, 161
Water, 120, 121
Watermelon Butterfly Salad, 129, 163
Wax beans, 95
Weight, 155
Wheat bran, 147
Whey, 103
Whipped cream, 107–108
  experiment, 108
  nutrients in, 162
  recipe, 109
Whipping, 8, 78, 169
Whisking, 8, 169
White Bread, 65–66, 161

White rice, 150–152
White sugar, 136, 140
Whole-grain bread, 33, 72
Whole-wheat bread, 72
Whole-Wheat Muffins, 77
Wild rice, 151
Winter Fruit Salad, 58, 160
Wire rack, 6
Wire whip, 6, 78
Wooden spoon, 6
Worcestershire sauce, 106

Yeast
  active dry, 65
  definition of, 61, 72, 169
  growing experiment, 64
  proofing, 62
Yogurt, 104, 157
Yogurt Dressing, 92
Yogurt Fruisicles, 123, 162
Yogurt Sundae, 110